The Pizza Equation

Slicing Up How to Run a Successful Pizza Enterprise

D1715353

Nick Bogacz

The Pizza Equation: Slicing Up How to Run a Successful Pizza
Enterprise
© 2019
By Nick Bogacz

All rights reserved. Reproduction or translation of any part of this
book through any means without permission of the copyright owner is
unlawful, except for promotional use. Request for other permissions or
further information should be addressed in writing to the publisher.

ISBN: 9781793204943

Editor: Gina Mazza (www.ginamazza.com)
Cover Design: Lee Ann Fortunato-Heltzel (www.creativeonemarket-
ing.com)
Cover Photography: Christina Keiser
Interior Photography: Frank Tunis

Nick Bogacz
Pittsburgh, PA
www.thepizzaequation.com
www.pizzadrafthouse.com

Praise for *The Pizza Equation* and Nick Bogacz

In the pizza industry, you meet all types of people, but none more experienced or inspirational than Nick Bogacz. In this book, he delves deep inside our industry's most challenging issues. The Pizza Equation is a must read for any operator.

–*Tony Gemignani, 13-time World Pizza champion, chef, master instructor, author and owner of Tony's Pizza Napoletana, Capo's, Pizza Rock, Slice House, Little Tony's, Tony's Coal Fire, Giovanni Italian Specialties and International School of Pizza*

Nick's business vision has made him an accomplished name in the pizza industry. His story and his many successes inspire pizzaiolos everywhere.

–*Scott Anthony, World Pizza champion, author, consultant and owner of Punxy Pizza*

From the beginning, Nick and the Caliente team have played an invaluable role in our city's flourishing craft beer scene. They are well versed in the product and have a unique understanding of the ever-evolving craft beer consumer.

–*Rob Soltis, Executive Editor, Craft Pittsburgh Magazine*

Nick is always doing great things for his team and to elevate the pizza industry as a whole. He is committed to self-improvement while empowering his team to think bigger, always bringing an army to food shows to allow them to grow. As an industry leader, he gives back to the pizza community through seminars and great reads like this one.

–*Jeremy Galvin, President, Master Pizza Franchise Group, LLC*

It's an indescribable feeling to experience a brand for the first time and know instantly that you're part of something special. This is how I felt the first time I visited Caliente Pizza & Draft House in Bloomfield, PA. As a loyal advocate of the independent beer scene, as well as a lover of all things pizza, I can say that Caliente had everything I could ask for thanks to Nick's vision. He understands where the beer world is headed, and it's not all about promo girls and pitcher specials—but rather, offering a diverse selection of beers from independent brands worldwide, tapping a keg of a rare beer and seeing how quickly enthusiasts lined up to enjoy. Nick's successful approach to building a beer program—paired with extraordinary, creative and downright delicious pizzas—has created a recipe for success that's allowed the Caliente brand to grow from one destination to five in just six years. The first line of the first feature I wrote for Caliente was a quote from Nick: "All I wanted to do was make great pizza." Staying true to this has helped him blaze an incredible trail through the pizza industry that includes rapid expansion, countless partnerships and relationships, and now a book where his success can be shared with other entrepreneurs. I am proud to call Nick a colleague, a business partner and, most importantly, a friend. His success is well deserved.

–*Jason M. Cercone, Founder of Breaking Brews, breakingbrews.com*

Every time I talk to Nick he seems to be opening a new restaurant. He's the real deal when it comes to entrepreneurship; he truly knows what it takes to open, operate and grow a restaurant. If you're looking to learn from someone who has actually done it, Nick's your guy.

–*Bruce Irving, Founder of SmartPizzaMarketing.com and named "Top 30 Restaurant Experts to Follow" for 2017 and 2018*

I was privileged to meet Nick and members of Caliente Pizza & Draft House years ago at a pizza competition. I was immediately impressed by their prowess in the pizza kitchen, as well as their fun-loving attitudes. Since then, I have witnessed Nick and his staff continually challenge themselves to be better every year. Winning trophies from numerous

national pizza competitions is one thing, but it's also how Nick and his team relate to the industry. Nick is one of the best out there—approachable, knowledgeable and always raising the bar for independent pizzeria owners. He has secured his place on the pizza scene as a successful pizzaiolo in both the kitchen and office. Growing his restaurants to new heights and with great success, I am very excited to see what the future holds for Caliente. I am honored to call him a friend and colleague.
–**Brian Hernandez,** *Test Chef for PMQ Pizza Magazine and US Pizza Team Director*

Nick has become one of the most successful independent pizzeria operators in America. His enthusiasm for and dedication to the craft have made Caliente Pizza & Draft House a favorite destination for pizza lovers in western Pennsylvania. I'm fortunate to count him amongst my pizza friends, and Pittsburgh is fortunate to have him making pizzas in such a great city.
–**Jeremy White,** *Editor in Chief, Pizza Today Magazine*

A class act. This phrase describes Nick's mission and his success thus far. Now a book! His commitment to quality is evident in the five shops he's opened in six years, his three-time world championships and a crew that smiles as much as he does. He makes good food in a comfortable atmosphere and his guests can rinse it down with the best craft beers around. God bless Nick and his work family. They make me proud to be part of the "pizza equation!"
–**Nino Sunseri,** *purveyor of pizzas and specialty Italian food supplies for over 50 years*

Dedication

To my dad, Bill Bogacz, who will never get a chance to read this book but who made me into the successful man I am today.

Contents

Introduction

If you are an entrepreneur who enjoys the restaurant industry and are looking to build an enterprise with pizza, this book is for you. It slices up the most important aspects of operating a pizza business and serves them all to you in one hot, handy guide.

I feel honored and blessed to have built a successful 22-plus-year career in the pizza business. As I will share, I started from the ground up as a delivery boy and am now owner of five successful stores that have won prestigious awards in the pizza sector. Now it's my turn to share what I've learned and provide opportunities for other entrepreneurs and pizza aficionados like yourself so that you, too, can benefit from my experience. Together, I can help you assemble the basic ingredients of the pizza business and build your own recipe for success. This book is designed with that goal in mind: To assist pizza enterprise owners in finding ways to stand out in the pizza-tossing crowd, be profitable and have a lot of fun doing it.

Whether you aspire to own one store or 10, one thing is always the same: It all starts with that first store, which will more than likely always be your baby. Even as you grow your restaurant family, you will forever have a special place in your heart for that firstborn store. I know I do, for these reasons: That first store is the one where I spent the most time. I cut my teeth there, formulated my recipes, improvised my vision and generally left it all on the table.

My philosophy with my first store should be your philosophy with yours: *This is my shot and no matter what, I will not fail.* That sounds simple and maybe cliché; however, it's an effective motivator. I didn't care if it took 18-hour days for a year straight. All I cared about was making it and, to me, that equated to being able to pay off all my business loans. It seemed like an eternity at the time but in actuality, it took four years to pay off the first store. I attribute it all to hard work and that "no-matter-what-this-will-work" attitude.

In Part 1, I open the book with a serving of pizza's illustrious history, as well as some background on how I got started in this industry that has happily consumed me as much as I enjoy consuming the product. It all began when I was a teenager who just wanted to drive around in my car delivering pizzas.

In Part 2, I serve up the most essential ingredients in running a successful pizza enterprise. It starts with building and leading a great team, structuring your internal management system, always choosing high quality ingredients for your products, and knowing your way around the branding, marketing and promotion game. I also share my best practices for becoming a contributing influence in your community's pride and your local region. To me, the best pizza stores are ones that embrace the culture of the area and create an entertaining relationship among their staff, clientele and community.

In Part 3, I describe how we were able to make a complete conversion with a four-day turnaround. It's was amazing to watch a shop operate under one ownership and then four days later, reopen under new ownership. I also share the inside scoop on my team's foray into the world of international pizza expos, as well as craft beer purveyorship. I end with my best tips for pizza business success and some additional resources for you to investigate beyond reading this book.

Pizza is meant to be shared, and so is my equation. I am proud and excited to do so. Enjoy and best wishes for your own success in this fast-paced, fun and delicious business!

PART 1:
HISTORY OF THE HUMBLE PIE

1

Best Cuts from Pizza's History

Fresh oven-baked crust slathered with juicy tomato sauce and spices, choice toppings piled high, all oozing with cheesy goodness. Pizza takes the plate as one of the most loved prepared food items of all times. When the craving for this humble pie hits, nothing else can substitute.

It's difficult to imagine a time when pizza was not a staple in the American diet. It's one of the most commonly shared meals because it is delicious, satisfying, inexpensive, highly customizable and easy to serve. It crops up everywhere there is a celebration, sporting event, friend gathering, family night or any reason at all. Let's say your son or daughter brings home a great report card or passes their driver's test. Time for pizza as a reward for a job well done! Your college buddies are in town and want to get together. It's only natural that you pick a local pizza shop and share a pie with your favorite beers on tap.

And who can resist pizza's hearty appeal when it can also be defended as a balanced, healthy meal choice? A key phytonutrient found in tomato sauce is lycopene. According to the Health Sciences Institute, this potent antioxidant can help prevent cancer and protect against heart disease. A study by the University of Arizona found that adding oregano to your pizza sauce can further boost immunity. Another great thing about pizza is that you don't need to make five different meals to get your recommended daily dietary intake. The major food groups (fruit, vegetables, dairy, lean meat and grains) can all be covered in this one awesome entrée.

Pizza is such an integral part of our national culture that Americans consume approximately 100 acres of pizza each day, or 350 slices per second. Each man, woman and child in the United States eats an average of 46 slices (23 pounds) of pizza a year. Approximately three billion pizzas are sold in the U.S. each year, and Italian food ranks as the most popular ethnic food in America. According to a recent Gallup Poll, children between the ages of three to 11 prefer pizza over all other food choices for lunch and dinner.

The Origin of Pizza

So how did pizza come to be? Okay, we know that it was invented by the Italians. The very first crust smothered with sauce and toppings was served in 1889 to honor the Queen Consort of Italy, Margherita of Savoy. Neapolitan chef Raffaele Esposito created the Pizza Margherita, garnished with red tomatoes, white mozzarella and green basil to represent Italy's national colors.

Yet the Italians weren't the only ones to throw the dough. Similar open pies date back even farther to ancient times. The Greeks, Egyptians, Armenians, Israelis and Babylonians and indigenous peoples from various geographic regions were making precursors to pizza by baking flatbread in mud ovens. This tasty meal of flatbread dough heaped with delicious toppings was worthy of being transported to all cultures and corners of the world and eventually created the now classic meal.

When the recipe for pizza pie was first brought across the Atlantic Ocean, it soon became a favorite on the North American continent. Approximately four million immigrants from southern Italy led the way in the early 20th Century by bringing their recipes with them when they arrived in the United States. The first official American pizzeria, Lombardi's, was opened in 1905 by Gennaro Lombardi at his Italian neighborhood grocery store on Spring Street in New York City.

Pizza shops continued to spring up throughout New York, New Jersey and up into New England in the early 1900s, according to Ed Levine's book, *Pizza: A Slice of Heaven*. "In 1912, Joe's Tomato Pies opened in Trenton, New Jersey," he writes. "Twelve years later, Anthony Totonno Pero left Lombardi's to open Totonno's in Coney Island. A year later, in 1925, Frank Pepe opened his eponymous pizzeria in New Haven, Connecticut. In 1929, John Sasso left Lombardi's to open John's Pizza in Greenwich Village. The 1930s saw this pie recipe spread to Boston (Santarpio's in 1933) and San Francisco with the opening of Tommaso's (1934), followed shortly thereafter with additional openings in New Jersey (Sciortino's in Perth Amboy in 1934 and the Reservoir Tavern in Boonton in 1936). In 1943, Chicago pizza was born when Ike Sewell opened Uno's. What did New York, New Haven, Boston and Trenton have in common? Their customer base: factory workers."

The mainstreaming of pizza into American life began in earnest after World War II, when American GIs stationed in Italy returned home with a hunger for the delicacy they had enjoyed overseas. In 1945, one of those returning soldiers, Ira Nevin, combined his eating experiences during the war with his expertise in repairing brick ovens for his father's oven-building business in The Bronx, New York. The result was the creation of the first gas-fired ceramic deck pizza oven. The brand, Baker's Pride Oven Company, is still in business today. This invention created quite a sizzle for pizza. The ovens are cleaner and more efficient than the earlier brick and coal ovens; and since they could easily be mass produced, America witnessed the industrialization of what would become our favorite savory pie.

Between 1945 and 1960, pizzerias continued to rise all over U.S. Most owners were independent operators—some Italian, others Greek, but all of them American. The remarkable model of buying local and using all fresh ingredients was at its peak. Pizza makers either made their own mozzarella or bought it fresh from a local grocery. Their scratch sauces were made from either fresh or canned tomatoes. Toppings were sourced from the neighborhood, as well, and created according to local clientele requests—making it one of the first truly craft foods. Pre-packaged crusts would have been a sacrilege; dough was always made and expertly tossed in house. Now that we are a fast food nation, we are finally getting wise and returning to this efficient and delicious way of cultivating and using our food resources. Even now, of all the abundant grab-and-go items available in the marketplace, pizza stands above them all as the most hearty, nutritious and fun food choice.

Yet pizzerias have become more than just places to get a good meal. They evolved into places where community residents could commune at the end of the work day or visit with each other as an alternative to eating at home. I guess you could say that they were (and still are to some extent) what today's coffeehouses have become as far as neighborhood gathering places.

The Rise of Pizza Franchises

After the craving for this simple dish started to take hold during the middle of the 20th Century, the pizza industry changed forever with the introduction of franchise businesses, or "chain stores." Pizza Hut was the first to hit the scene; it was founded in Wichita, Kansas in 1958. Little Caesar's emerged in 1959 and Domino's in 1960 (both in Michigan), and Papa John's opened in 1984 in Indiana. This was a new and different kind of business model for pizzerias. The goal, of course, was to make a profit utilizing the well-loved pizza as the main product. What created a culture shift in the industry was a focus on producing inexpensive products that could easily be replicated in other chain locations.

This franchise business model turned the pizza pie food product into a commodity. Pizzas were made by hand, so they could still be marketed as "hand made" but the sauce, cheese and dough ingredients were produced in a central location then shipped to each pizza store. These chain pizza shops basically sold inexpensive communal food with a fun image. As they increased in popularity, many of the existing mom-and-pop pizza shops began to have difficulty competing with the low-priced products served up by the franchises. Independent owners couldn't buy ingredients in bulk quantities so their production costs were higher. In response, many strived to maintain high quality levels but their ability to dominate their market space was being gobbled up by the chains that touted an affordable version of this treat delivered quickly and piping hot right to your door.

Today, there is obviously a need being served by pizza franchises. With so many pizza restaurants available throughout the country, eating this meal has become even more of an easy habit for Americans. For parents seeking ways to inexpensively feed their families, frequenting a favorite chain pizza shop fits the bill. For diehard pizza aficionados, however, there is nothing better than patronizing the locally owned-and-operated shops that boast of handmade selections comprised of fresh, wholesome ingredients. In such establishments, the recipes are creatively crafted and highly customizable. So how do you find these icon eateries if you're not from the area? Ask the local residents for suggestions about their hidden gems (they will certainly be able to recommend the culinary pride of their neighborhood) or look up recommendations on Yelp, Facebook, Google Reviews, Instagram and OpenTable. Depending on the town you're in, residents may even take you there to share a taste of their specialty! It seems like every community has its own pizzeria, many of which are beloved landmarks in the area.

What I find particularly interesting about this industry is its regional flavor. Wherever I travel for business or pleasure, I make it a point to try the local pizza. There are definite differences. In New York, you can get a slice of pizza with what the natives say is the best crust. It's thick and crisp only along its edge yet soft, thin and pliable enough beneath its toppings to be folded in half. This texture allows for large slices that can be consumed on the go, as any New Yorker will tell you. When I'm in Chicago, I find that their deep-dish pie is best eaten with a knife and fork. Detroit boasts the rectangular pan-baked pizza that has a thick, crisp crust and toppings like pepperonis and mushrooms. In California, I find a variety of fresh vegetables topping crispy pizzas.

I have discovered that people all over America vehemently support their local pizzas with as much gusto as supporting their local sports teams. Here in Pittsburgh where I'm based, I do the same. In this City of Champions, we bring much passion and loyalty to our local teams and our approach to pizza making is no less dedicated and discerning. Our Caliente restaurants feature the unique Pittsburgh pizza style that the locals have come to know and love. When in the 'Burgh, you've got to savor this mouthwatering pie with a light, airy crust, freshly made tomato sauce and a bubbly blanket of mozzarella and provolone cheeses. The Caliente business model is based on producing the best quality product and serving it up in a style that reflects the tastes of the local culture. The model is based on reinvigorating an existing store into a thriving community eatery with a consistent menu of quality food, excellent customer service, and ambiance. It is our aspiration that with each restaurant we transform, we will create an icon for the community. Our vision is to come full circle with recreating those earliest pizza shops and serve as favored local eateries for people to gather and make good memories.

No Pie in the Sky

It's clear that being successful in the pizza business is not a pie-in-the-sky notion. Today, it's a $41 billion industry with more than 75,000 pizza restaurants in the United States alone. These restaurants make up 17 percent of all restaurants in America—and that percentage, like dough, is still on the rise. In fact, pizza was unsurprisingly labeled as the fastest growing segment of fast-casual restaurants in 2018 by the Pizza Power Report in *PMQ Pizza Magazine*. The popularity of pizza does not diminish even in a wobbly economy. Consumer taste for it never wanes. On any given day, about 13 percent of Americans eat pizza, consuming a average of 350 slices per second! It's safe to say that this food item will stay hot in the oven for a very long time into the future.

2
My Love Affair
with Pizza

I'll say up front that the pizza business can be grueling, but I love it like
nothing else I've ever done and I wouldn't change a thing. My involvement in the pizza industry started in 1996 as a delivery driver. Over the
years, I've worked my way to the top of the organizational food chain
by being hired as a pizza maker, assistant general manager and general
manager. During my pizza career, I was employed by six different organizations before becoming an entrepreneur and shop owner. With each
one, I learned different slices of the pizza business circle.

What's funny is that I didn't originally set out to be a pizza entrepreneur. As I started to raise a family with my wife, Angie, I experimented
with working a few "real jobs." Still, there was only a brief period of
time when I didn't have some involvement in the pizza world.

I lasted only six months selling advertising for a local radio station.
I took that 9-to-5 position after returning to my native Pittsburgh from
Wilkes Barre, Pennsylvania. I'd been working as a general manager for
a national pizza chain, putting in 70 to 80 hours a week. My heavy work
schedule was interfering with my ability to be a hands-on dad to my two
children, who were ages five and three at the time.

Shortly after I landed the job at the radio station, I discovered that

I didn't like being cooped up in an office. That's when I started delivering pizzas for my friend, Ozzie, two days a week, just for some extra income. His shop, Captain's Pizza, was close to where my family had relocated in the suburbs—literally right across the street from my house. Captain's Pizza was my first experience with an independent shop; up until then, all the other positions were at franchise stores. Then I called Sam, another friend who was managing a national franchise in downtown Pittsburgh and started delivering pizza for him two days a week.

So now I was up to delivering four days a week. I was rolling in a bit more dough for my family but even more so, I realized how much I loved and missed the industry. Pizza is fun! Everybody loves it. Whenever I'd make advertising sales calls at the radio station, I'd usually get the cold shoulder; but every time I delivered pizzas to a home or business, the reaction was the opposite:

"Hey, the pizza guy's here! Yay!"

People were happy to see me and I loved bringing joy to them in this simple way. Providing pizza to social gatherings, family outings and company celebrations always seems to be a positive experience.

So before too long, I found myself right back in the pizza business full time. Angie was worried that we would find ourselves in the same predicament that I left in Wilkes Barre, working my tail off and never seeing my family. That's when I figured, you know what, I'm going to go be a mailman. I went to the post office and took the test and passed it. I was hired for a full time position but continued to deliver pizzas for Ozzie and Sam four days a week.

The very first day I worked at the post office I could tell that this was where people's dreams went to die. I had the same dilemma there as with the radio station: Delivering mail was nothing like delivering pizza. I would arrive at six o'clock in the morning and sort mail for two to three hours then deliver the mail for as long as it took; but I delivered to mail boxes, not people. There was no cheering like when I'd deliver pizza. In fact, it was a thankless job of long hours in solitude. That could be my life but I knew I wouldn't be satisfied. I could continue this postal job and work in a passionless situation for the next 35 years until I retired, or I could go back to doing what I loved.

During my tenure at the post office, a fellow employee, John, noticed that I was a good worker and wanted to know if I would count money for the concession stands at the Civic Arena, the former home of the Pittsburgh Penguins, in my extracurricular time. So, I fit that work in during the evenings when events were in town. In the meantime, Ozzie had opened a second shop and I began delivering pizzas for that shop, so I went from holding down three jobs to five jobs—which I kept up for two years at over 85 hours a week.

Managing a Profitable Pizza Franchise

That's when an owner of the national franchise I was delivering for approached me about taking Sam's job. In the pizza world, you get to know everybody, especially with so many different franchises. So, in this case, the franchise store was struggling but Sam was a good friend of mine, and I refused to take his job. They put in somebody else. Another nine months went by and the owners came back to me indicating that they were firing Sam's replacement. I didn't know this person as well so it didn't feel like I'd be taking a job from a friend. (Later on, I was reconnected with this manager and we've become good friends to this day.) I figured, at that point, that I could take my five jobs and maybe maneuver them into two.

So, I told the owner, "You know, look, I'm working at the post office. Hey, I can't guarantee you I'm going to work as your general manager for 50, 60, 70 or 80 hours a week as I have in the past in similar positions. I'm already working 40 to 50 hours at the post office so I can take this job and be your general manager, but I never want to hear how many hours I have to put in. But it will be done right in the amount of time I have to give, which is probably between 42 and 45 hours per week."

So, the owners hired me as general manager of the pizza shop franchise, and I kept the post office job. I stopped delivering pizza for Ozzie's two shops and counting money at the arena. I quickly learned the skill of delegation. That became one of the keys to my success, which I'll delve into a bit later in the book.

When I started managing that store, I focused on boosting sales. The previous year it had gross revenues of $750,000 and a net profit of $27,000. After my first year as manager, we were raking in a million dollars in gross revenue and $148,000 in net profit. It was the first time in its 20-year history of hitting one million in sales. Obviously, that was a huge deal and I achieved this while working a full schedule of schlepping through the streets delivering mail.

After that first year, I went to the owners and offered a suggestion that would allow me to rid myself of the post office job and work solely in the pizza business. I requested a raise in salary commensurate to my post office salary. They looked at my proposed number and declined. The owners were savvy businessmen who owned many successful food franchises. They responded that if I were to leave, they would just simply sell the company, which they did six months after I left. That's when I got serious about opening my own pizza shop (more about that in a minute). I could have worked for that franchise full time, probably for the rest of my career, and be happy, but I wanted more.

Looking back, I am thankful for all of my previous work experiences in other jobs because the knowledge I learned still helps me today. For example, when sending out direct mail flyers to residents, I use my experience as a postal worker to identify which zip codes to choose and how the mail delivery process works. I know how to purchase radio advertising and write 30-second spots. By working in six different pizza enterprises over the course of my career, I've had the opportunity to learn every sector of the business. Yet I realized that something was missing during my experience with each company: The company wasn't mine. I was always working for somebody else. I started to realize that as I was providing for my family, I was also building business profits for the pizza shop owner. Eventually, I was ready to take a big risk and go into business for myself. It was time for me to cut out my slice of the pizza pie industry.

The Creation of Caliente

So I decided that if I'm going to do pizza for life, then I'm going to do pizza for my family and me. I started walking into independently owned pizza shops around the well-trafficked Oakland area of Pittsburgh, where the University of Pittsburgh is located, and asking the owners if they might be interested in selling. The first four told me to get the hell out. The fifth guy I approached wanted to talk. His friend had a pizza shop in Bloomfield, known as Pittsburgh's Little Italy. When I walked in I saw what predominantly looked like a bar that happened to have a full pizza kitchen in the back. We sat down to look at the numbers, and they made sense; so just like that, we bought the store. For the next six months, I kept saying that all I wanted was a pizza shop and nothing more. The bar, little did I know, was a blessing in disguise.

Angie and I purchased that first store in September 2012. We had intended to change the name but we built up the brand so quickly that we instead decided to keep the original "Caliente" part and change the "bar" reference to "Pizza & Draft House." One of the two previous owners, Taner Nalbant, who is Turkish, would blush when I'd ask him why he chose the Caliente name. After some prodding, he told me that he named his joint after the top strip club in Turkey. With a hand shake and no monies exchanged, I took over the store, ran it for nine months then gave Taner all of the money we were able to save up while running the business during those nine months, along with a small loan from my parents. Taner and his partner Danny held the remainder of the note for five years, and the rest is history!

It was to be the first of five stores we eventually debuted in the Pittsburgh area. When we opened our doors at that Bloomfield location, my mission was to be part of inspiring a movement to re-instill pride in the pizza maker's craft. Handcrafted quality can't be overstated, and I understood the importance of using fresh ingredients rather than frozen and pre-packaged products. Consistently high-quality ingredients and excellent customer service had to be something our clientele could rely on—both in the restaurant and behind our bar counters.

Our flagship Bloomfield location was my first experience owning and operating a bar. I dove into the opportunity head on, pouring over books and websites, researching craft beers and learning the best practices for managing a bar. At that location, we now offer more than 140 hand-selected craft beer varieties with 20 varieties on tap, along with a unique selection of personally designed craft cocktails.

The Caliente family has grown as our business has grown. When we opened in 2012, it was just Angie and me. I worked the kitchen and she worked the front of the house. As our store grew, we added a cook and a waitress. Delivery drivers and bartenders were soon to follow in the hiring process. Our flagship Bloomfield store was followed by a second one in my hometown of Hampton, located north of the city. We then expanded to a third location in an upscale town south of the city called Mt. Lebanon, which has a very different feel from the other two.

It became evident even as we opened store number four in a sleepy borough along the Allegheny River that we were onto something. Store number five opened in early 2019 in a booming town east of the city.

The growth of the Caliente business has intentionally grown slowly and steadily over the years to ensure great customer service and the best food possible. Each store has its own atmosphere partly because we purchased pre-existing shops and converted them to the Caliente brand. The whole conversion process is a story of its own, and we'll be talking about that in Part 3. I will give you a hint: I watched a lot of episodes of Bar Rescue featuring Jon Taffer, who converts failing bars into thriving enterprises.

The Caliente store in Hampton retains its original patio
as part of its unique character.

Success One Slice at a Time

The equation for building a successful pizza enterprise is very straightforward. The industry is centered on the pizza pie, which is easy to make, transport and consume. So, it seems like anyone could be successful making such a simple dish. Yet, beneath the bubbly cheese and delicious toppings is the real ingenuity.

As an entrepreneur who has achieved my goals and then some, I want to emphasize that there is no such thing as overnight success. To get to the position where I could buy my own pizza shop and expand in several locations, I had to put in a lot of long hours of sweat and hard work. Being a pizza man has been a rewarding experience. When I was holding down those delivery jobs with three local pizza shops earlier in my career, I knew I would always do what it takes to support and care for my family. It has provided the economic means for raising my family and pride in being part of a great American tradition.

PART 2:
THE INGREDIENTS OF A SUCCESSFUL PIZZA ENTERPRISE

3

Foundational Dough: Build a Great Team

In the pizza business, there is one main goal: Give customers a piping hot pizza that they can't resist. Whether your venture is an eat-in shop or delivery only, each pie must spring from the oven in a reasonable amount of time. After all, a pizza craving doesn't quit; it only intensifies!

Doing this successfully takes a team effort. There is something about working in a pizza shop that just brings out team spirit. That's, of course, if you have good management. The culture stems from the top down. Having a well-coordinated organization that is team-oriented makes working at a pizza shop fun and motivating.

As I stated earlier, my first job in the pizza industry was as a delivery boy but it wasn't my first experience with building a team and learning about effective leadership. Those lessons came much earlier in my life through another means: sports.

What Sports Taught Me About Teamwork

Let me diverge a little to tell you about my experience with youth sports and how it influenced my leadership style. I grew up with a brother who is seven years older than me, and two brothers who are four and six years younger. We had a local youth foundation within walking distance of our house and we were very active in it. I played every form of recreation that the foundation offered. I was never good enough to be on any high school teams, but that really wasn't my desire. I preferred being a coach, so that's what I did. I was my two younger brothers' coach when I was only 12 years old and I developed strong leadership skills that I didn't even realize I had until years later in my career.

I also learned the value of practice. My younger brothers were on competitive tournament baseball teams and we'd practice for hours while our dad was at work. We'd go to the ball field and I'd pitch to my brothers. I would correct them on their batting stances and other details. I picked up everything I could find about Major League Baseball player skills in sports magazines, by watching ESPN's SportsCenter and from youth coaches in the area, and we would practice all of them. As a result, both of my younger brothers went onto play for high school teams.

I also became a youth hockey team coach when I was 12 years old. (That was a big year for me!) I would hold practices for the kids on Friday nights. The players would come down to the gym, where I had cones set up for passing and weaving drills. We'd talk about strategies for our upcoming competitions. The first year that I coached the team, we took the championship. We continued to do so in the years to come. I earned such a good reputation that the kids always wanted to be on my team because of the way I ran the practices and training, and how I helped the players instill respect for one another.

Looking back, I think that the parents appreciated it, too, because a lot of times when you get into these tournament teams, the coaches are screaming at the kids about stuff like mental toughness. I taught the players about good sportsmanship. Even though I was ultra-competitive, my teams had the most fun. I didn't realize how much I was being an effective leader because at that age, I wasn't thinking in those terms. At age 14, I was named a "volunteer of the month" at the youth foundation. My name is still on a plaque there. That experience meant so much to me and I still think of it as my first job. I loved volunteering down there and I think that what I learned so early on still has a lot to do with my ability to notice what it takes to build a great team. I took all of this into my pizza career.

My First Pizza Team Experiences

When I started in the pizza industry as a driver at age 17 for a shop near my home, I immediately loved it. What teenager wouldn't want that job? You get to drive around in your car and listen to sports and music all night. But it wasn't all fun and games. Soon after I started at that job, I wrecked my car. No injuries, thank goodness, but I was left with no car. This could have been the end of my pizza delivery career but by the following Friday, my mom had loaned me her vehicle and was back to work. Unfortunately, I had another minor fender bender with her car, so the manager brought me inside to work the ovens. I guess he figured I'd be better at baking than steering.

So as it turned out, that setback was a blessing because I was promoted to pulling pizzas from the ovens and routing the drivers. I loved that job. I quickly got good at routing and helping the drivers make excellent time and tip money. I also learned a lot about what it takes to make good pizza. Once I mastered pizza making, the ovens and the hoagie line, I moved up to shift manager. By the time I was 19 years old, I was overseeing all the guys making pizzas and hoagies on the food line. From there I continued to work my way up the company ladder, which is possible to do in the pizza chain industry.

Naturally, I carried my lessons learned in sports team leadership into the pizza parlor. I continued to experience that the great thing about having a good team atmosphere is that everyone is motivated to get the work done, and done well. There were 25 of us in this shop, and we all worked collaboratively to get the orders out. Each person knew what his or her job responsibility was in the pizza-making process and our hours in the kitchen were finely choreographed for this reason. We didn't step on each other's toes; we worked in synch and took pride in our respective parts of the process.

Since that very first job in the pizza shop, I have run across lots of interesting characters in this business. Everyone has their special areas of expertise and throughout my career, I have learned from all of them. I'd like to share a few stories about some of my favorite co-workers over the years. At that first pizza job, the general manager was named Ufuk (he was originally from Turkey). He was driven and motivated to make the shop a success. Ufuk built great team spirit by always helping out where needed. For example, he always pitched in to work the pizza ovens on Friday nights when it was super busy. At some point along the way, Ufuk realized that his name could be misinterpreted in the worst possible way—as an expletive! To avoid any confusion or possible insults, he refused to sign his name (as is customarily done) on the bottom of the order slips delivered with the pizzas. Instead, he wanted anyone who had a problem with an order to call the shop and ask for Tony.

John, the second general manager at that same shop, was the "fixer." When Ufuk relocated to Virginia, the franchise organization brought in John to improve the shop's revenue and overall success. He eliminated subpar staff and hired new staff to offer better service. John was excellent at marketing strategies. In fact, we still use some of them today at Caliente, such as sending staff out into the neighborhoods to distribute door hangers (this always boosts sales).

Jim was that same shop's third general manager. He was excellent at restaurant management strategies, including the most effective ways to keep the store clean. That may seem trivial, as though there are no unique skills involved, but let's think about cleaning for a moment. Cleaning the pizza shop is a good example of learning from one another and working as a team. You always clean from the top down. That's what Jim taught me. With cleaning, everyone lends a hand. Obviously, in the kitchen, cleaning takes on a higher level of consideration. We wiped things down continuously and were very careful about washing hands, sanitizing and keeping ingredients in their proper storage locations. Even at Caliente today, the cleaning responsibilities are listed on several job description checklists and we coach our younger workers on how to pay attention to these details. A good manager communicates the importance of everyone pitching in. When the shop is humming and busy, it's all hands on deck. If someone needs a hand in the kitchen, you pitch in. Whoever has a spare moment checks the restrooms and does a quick sweep of the floor.

Becoming General Manager at Age 21

Company teams are successful for one reason: The company is in business to make a profit; but to make a profit, you have to have people who are good at making great food and delivering excellent customer service. This core team establishes an atmosphere in which people want to come back for more great food and excellent service.

The first time I was a general manager, I learned this firsthand. This experience of being responsible for running the shop occurred at the second pizza franchise where I was employed. This franchise owner taught me the financial side of the business. I saw the numbers and learned what they meant. He had everything detailed to show how much we were spending on pepperoni and cheese, utilities, napkins and condiments, and even toilet paper. Everything was spelled out in a ledger book that he shared with me. I learned that just because you sell pizzas for 10 bucks each, it doesn't mean you're making $9.99 in profit. I learned that a lot of other costs contribute to the sale of that pizza.

That position at the second pizza franchise was one of my highest paid jobs in my career as an employee and I was young, only 21 years old. In fact, I was too young to be as effective as I should have been running a shop. Being as young as the workers that I was supervising made it difficult for me to build a solid team atmosphere. The staff didn't have the same motivation as the workers at my former job and they didn't respect me because I was "one of them." The goal of making a great pizza and getting it out the door quickly was not their focus.

Still, I watched what the older managers did when they were at the shops and how they presented themselves. I learned that if you want to gain respect you have to give respect. To this day, I always walk into a store and if I see someone I don't know working there, I introduce myself and learn the person's name. Small gestures go a long way. People are always watching you and how you handle yourself. Applying life rules—like treating others the way you want to be treated—goes a long way. I was lucky enough to observe managers and supervisors using these social skills from a young age and I learned to never underestimate the power of the words "please" and "thank you."

Another lesson that became crystal clear to me from these early experiences as a general manager is that the owner must know the reason why he or she is in business, and that reason must be conveyed to the staff. Aside from turning a profit, for instance, the owner may want to produce the best pizzas or be a pillar in the community. At the second franchise where I worked, the owner had bought it as an investment and really didn't know the pizza business. He was not as concerned about creating a great product or providing superior customer service. His sole reason for owning the shop was to turn as big a profit as possible. I didn't yet have the leadership skills that I'd eventually come to acquire and the owner was not concerned about helping me build a healthy work culture. I was failing miserably at my general manager position and I knew it. The irony of the situation wasn't lost on me: The owner was purely focused on profit but without a highly productive, cohesive team, he was barely making enough to stay in business.

Along with learning the financial aspects of the business in this general manager position, I learned something else, as well: humility. I was let go. The owner knew he was going to shut down the store and wanted me to learn from the experience without feeling that the time was a loss. I did learn. I learned a lot. I incorporated what he taught me about the financial side of the business into the shops that I managed going forward. I learned the value of strong leadership and what happens when these skills are absent. It's a crucial part of what has helped form the Pizza Equation philosophy.

Building a Pizza Franchise Team

It was coming clear to me that a business is only as good as its people and the pizza industry is no exception. I've worked in a few privately owned pizza shops over the years but working in a franchise business provides a different perspective on building a team. Some of the pizza franchises follow a traditional corporate structure, where individuals start in lower paying positions like driver or server and work their way up the ladder to become a franchise store owner. It can be a great career!

Teamwork in these shops has a different flavor than privately owned ones. One example that I want to share describes the importance and benefits of building a healthy company culture within the franchise system, and the skills necessary to create a highly productive team.

Out in Wilkes Barre, Pennsylvania, I worked for a reputable and very successful franchise organization that had developed a truly inspiring company culture. Getting hired into that company took some effort by the franchise owners because I had to move my family there from Pittsburgh; however, they showed me the payroll numbers with bonuses included, so I seized this great opportunity to be the general manager.

Once on board, I soon learned that it was a great place to work. We had the advantage of being located in a college town, where pizza eaters are abundant but so are retail pizza options. I came into this already established franchise location as the sales builder. The store was doing sales of $16,000 a week when I arrived. By the time I left that position 18 months later, it was closer to $25,000 a week. I was still young, motivated and happy to be working for a rock-solid franchise. We expanded our closing time from two to four o'clock in the morning. We ran deliveries like it was nobody's business. We offered all kinds of delicious specials. Staff from some of the other franchise locations would come into my store, which served as the business headquarters, and drop off their paperwork on a Sunday night, and they'd find us doing the franchise cheer. Everything was upbeat and fun, even the phone message when customers called in to order.

When I assumed that general manager position, I quickly noticed the loyalty and allegiance among the employees. The team atmosphere was incredible. I met a driver who was an accountant by day and a deliveryman during the evening hours. He'd been driving for the franchise for 18 years and loved it. Another driver had just celebrated his 25-year anniversary with the company. Our workers wore T-shirts with their years of service displayed on the sleeves. From the corporate headquarters down through the franchise owners and store managers, the overall message conveyed was always positive and motivating. Employees were valued. Innovative ideas were encouraged. The corporate chant would erupt among the employees if we needed a boost after working long hours into the night.

I loved this sense of celebration and family camaraderie at the Wilkes Barre store. I knew then and I know now how important it is to have great team spirit. I continue to instill that sense of spirit in each Caliente shop. As I've stated already (yet it bears repeating), having a positive, supportive team atmosphere where respect is a central part of the culture is a core ingredient in building a successful pizza enterprise. Such spirit within the four walls of the building spills out into the community. It's where your marketing message begins: with the staff. It translates into having employees who actually look forward to coming to work and customers who look forward to coming into the stores. With that thought in mind, here are my highly recommended team-building strategies.

Team-Building Strategies

Award Your Top Performers. The store managers at our Caliente locations keep a tally of daily tasks that are completed by the employees. The checklist is like a scorecard. Completing it helps the managers monitor the completion of each employee's daily assignments. The stores also are reviewed weekly by our regional chef to make certain that all safety regulations, food handling and operating procedures are being appropriately carried out. After each week's reporting is submitted, the store with the highest tally number is given the "Caliente Store of the Week" trophy to display at the winning store location. Competition for the trophy encourages teamwork among the staff at the various locations.

Our "Caliente Store of the Week" trophy.

Motivate Your Drivers. One of the lessons I learned about selling boxes of pizza is that by motivating the drivers, I could sell more pizzas and bring in more revenue for the company. Here is an example. When we opened a new suburban store, I quickly found that I needed to boost sales. I was averaging $7,000 per week in sales. We established a sales strategy using three drivers who would take 30 pizzas—freshly baked from the oven—and visit big box stores, construction sites and hospitals at lunchtime. They would sell the boxed pizzas for $6 each. The drivers would keep $1 and the store would receive $5 for each pizza sold. If three drivers sold 30 pizzas per day, that would bring in $450 to the store per day, or $2,250 every week.

To motivate the drivers, I gave them restaurant gift cards to the local steak house every time they sold their 150 pizzas per week. It was an easy way to spread a little cheer in the corporate community and add 30 percent in revenues to our coffers. I also found a large carton of post-cards when I arrived at this suburban shop, so I went through the data-base and direct-mailed cards offering a $3 discount on their next order to all customers who had not purchased in the last 60 days.

A word about direct mail, while I'm on the subject: Back in the good old days, like 10 or 15 years ago, the best way to send direct mail would be to save customers' addresses in a database, print postcards, add post-age and mail them. That's exactly what I did when I took over the big chain I ran at the beginning of my career. Nowadays, it makes more sense to do these mailings in one of two ways: 1) Hire a direct mail mar-keting company to send them for you or 2) use the USPS' Every Door Direct Mailing program. I personally use a great company called Mail Shark. They mail 1,000 of my customers per store every week; and five times a year I change the content of the postcard. The benefit of doing direct mail as compared to being in coupon magazines or having a flyer inside a bundle of flyers is obvious: It is better seen because it stands alone in the mailbox. I love to print giant-sized postcards; this almost guarantees that all other mail for the day will be stuffed inside my direct mail piece, thereby making it the most visible item in any mailbox.

Host Company Celebrations. Caliente hosts a summer picnic and a Christmas party each year for all of our employees. It is similar to what

Good Cheer at the Calentie annual Christmas party.

I learned when working with the large franchise company that I speak about in this chapter. They would throw a huge holiday party for their staff and family members. It's important to invest in your people. We add our own flair to this team-building event and make it a point to celebrate the hard work and dedication delivered by our staff. These events also offer an opportunity for the five-store personnel to meld into one company culture. We want them to feel appreciated. We want to show them that they are part of something special, because they are!

Offer Professional Development. At Caliente, we offer ongoing professional development for our staff. Our employees can choose to climb the ladder in our organization. At the management level, we hold monthly training sessions to learn new leadership skills and discuss ways to motivate staff. There are some things that we talk about in every single meeting. We start the meetings the same way: by reading our mission statement and talking about LARK, which is the way we handle customer complaints (it's an acronym for Listen, Apologize, Resolve the issue and Keep the promise.) Every meeting I talk about PSI, or "product service and image." I want to make sure that we have the best products, the best service and the best company image. Product can be anything from the way you're putting your food out for delivery or pickup to how it's coming out of the ovens. I ask my staff, "Is it something you would serve your mother?" Good service can entail the way we answer the phones, the way the hostess greets patrons, the way our bus staff clears tables. Image is about how the store looks. Is all the signage lit? Is the staff in the right uniforms?

In addition to reviewing company procedures in these meetings, we have a topic of the month. It may be about communication, training new staff, or tending to details. The focus is always on staff improvement and growth. These meetings build camaraderie and boost morale. We also underwrite company trips to various pizza-making competitions and conferences. We encourage our management to participate at these events. It's been a big success for Caliente, as our staff members have won many industry awards. Participating in the Pizza Expo in Las Vegas is our favorite. More about that in an upcoming chapter!

4
Saucy, Cheesy Goodness: Top It Off with High Quality Ingredients

If you ask consumers what they like best about pizza, you'd probably get as many different answers as there are topping options. Behind the scenes in the pizza industry, a lot goes into creating a superior pie. One of the biggest concerns is always balancing price and quality; in other words, how to make the most delectable product at the lowest cost.

When I analyze any of the well-respected and long-running pizza enterprises that produce handmade fresh pizzas, I find that the owners have painstakingly taken time to experiment with and perfect their recipes and baking strategies. At Caliente, we are no different. When we opened our first pizza shop, I started from scratch to create our signature crust recipe and signature sauce recipe, and designated what toppings would be allowed to grace our pizzas. Our very own sauce calls for a specified type of tomato and our local vendor keeps us well supplied. Our cheese mixture requires the highest quality cheeses from the best available sources. Finally, our hand-prepared toppings create a pizza masterpiece. We taste-test everything and from the comments we receive, we determine the final versions of our culinary delights.

The various franchise chains where I've worked have had different opinions on the importance of quality, convenience and price. Some have determined that buying in bulk from a central distributor and shipping frozen pre-made food items for quick and easy production is the best business model to follow. At those locations, you can pick up a pie and feed your family inexpensively. So my then career consisted of taking ingredients out of bags and cans.

After being in the business for 16 years and before opening my own store, I knew what a great pizza tasted like and I was aware of what made each chain's recipe different. Just like you can hear a singer's voice and know that it's his or her song, I knew that when someone ate a Caliente pizza, I wanted it to taste like only my pizza and not even remotely like anyone else's.

To differentiate the taste of our signature pizzas, I decided to not use the same providers as all the other pizza shops in the area. I went to Pittsburgh's famous Strip District, where the freshest produce and Italian meats and cheeses are sold. I was introduced to the local legend Nino Sunseri, who ran a popular family Italian groceria called Sunseri Brothers and a wholesale food business. Nino told me from the beginning that he was not the cheapest price in town but he could source me the best quality ingredients of anyone around. So now I had a source for top-shelf ingredients with which to formulate our recipes.

Of course, there's a secret ingredient!

Creating a stellar pizza starts with not just that good foundational dough of building a great team, but literally creating good dough. So our dough recipe was the first signature item we perfected.

I started with a simple recipe and made it my own. We chose the best flour and olive oil available. We sprinkled in the sugar and salt. Then we tested the recipe with family and friends. The first week that we took over our first Caliente restaurant, we invited everyone to come and taste test our recipes. With my family there, I made my first dough batch and everyone tried it. They agreed that it was good . . . but only good, not great.

For my next batch, I consulted a good friend who had many years in the baking industry along with fine dining experience. I showed my future Regional Chef Eric Von Hansen my recipe and asked him specifics about how to add in my ingredients to make the dough. Everyone agreed that this second batch was very good. It was very airy and did not fold when picked up; however, I was not convinced that it was different enough from everyone else's. That's when I had an epiphany that the dough was missing was a secret ingredient. I added it and did not tell anyone.

That made all the difference!! Nobody knew what I added but they tasted my third batch and said it was superb. It had all of the qualities of the second dough but with a unique flavor that put it over the top.

Consulting with the Sauce Lady

After I nailed the dough recipe, I moved onto perfecting my signature sauce. Nino sent over his "sauce lady", a very nice woman from Stanislaus Tomato Company. I tried many different tomato bases. Not wanting to taste like anyone else's pizza, I stayed true to that theme and picked a chunky sauce for our everyday sauce. I then called Nino and started to put together my own spice blend using only the best spices. After a few more taste tests with my family, they agreed that the sauce was excellent.

We did the same thing with our cheese choices. We kept trying different kinds until we found one that went perfectly with our sauce and dough: a blend from Grande Cheese Company in Wisconsin.

Once you experiment, taste test and settle on your unique sauce and cheese recipes, I suggest never changing them (which is why it's important to get them right up front!). There's nothing worse than going to your favorite restaurant and realizing that they changed their recipe. Whenever we do get the itch to alter one of our recipes—whether for the dough, sauce or cheese—we just add a whole new line of pizzas and keep the original recipes.

In the end, using fresh, high quality ingredients never goes out of style. In fact, they are the basis for all the other pizza fads that have come on the scene in recent years. So as you read further about the latest trends, keep in mind that it's the ingredients that make or break every one of them.

Artisan Trend

After days of taste-testing with our family, our signature Caliente Pepperoni Pizza recipe was born.

Artisanal food items are definitely a trend in the U.S.—or more like a movement—and that trend has found its way into the pizza segment of the food wheel. Some upscale pizzerias have opted for the artisan route where gourmet pizza choices are featured. This style of pizza, I believe, represents a consumer rebellion against the super inexpensive chains serving mass-produced food products.

More expensive to make and using higher quality products, customers are willing to pay more for the artisan style because it allows them to enjoy pies with interesting flavor combinations and nontraditional ingredients. Ten years ago, for example, pizzerias offered only one type of crust; now different varieties—including gluten-free, cauliflower and zucchini crusts—are all the rage in many pizzerias.

The same goes with cheeses. The once popular mozzarella, provolone and feta are getting a run for their cheesiness with aged, smoked and other craft-type choices—although a nice aged Parmigiano Reggiano is still our favorite on many of our specialty pizzas.

Other artisan trends include dessert pizza and even pickle pizzas. Yes, pickles! To start out your store in the artisan trend, it's best to find or create recipes that you love then perfect them before offering them on your menu.

Health Conscious Trend

In today's world, there is an increase in health consciousness among consumers and this interest has affected the pizza industry. I like to promote the nutritional value of pizza. It is a complete meal that offers essential dietary ingredients such as vegetables, dairy and whole grains.

Many pizza shops allow patrons to customize their orders by selecting thinner crusts made of whole grains, adding fruits, choosing leaner meats and extra vegetables, requesting vegan cheese or limiting the amount of cheese on their pies. If you do not use any animal products in your dough or sauce then you should offer and advertise it as a vegan option.

Regional Style Trend

Another popular trend and one that I love to both test and eat is the regional style pizzas from around the country. Years ago, two types dominated: Chicago style and New York style. Now various regional styles are popping up in many other geographic areas, including but not limited to Grandma style, Detroit pan pizzas, Roman style, St. Louis style and Old Forge style from northeastern Pennsylvania.

We offer a lot of regional styles at different times throughout the year at our restaurants. It gives our customers something to look forward to and another great special for us to promote. Rather than just marketing a new specialty pizza, we make a whole new style of regional pie that many in our area may not have had before but fall in love with at first bite.

Locally Sourced and Scratch Ingredients Trend

Like the chefs who make them, pizza connoisseurs don't toss the quality of their ingredients around lightly either. They respect the dough, the sauce and the toppings. It wouldn't be unusual for longtime pizza lovers to know the difference between a frozen, out-of-the-box impostor and a fresh pie that is custom-made in house from scratch ingredients. On top of being able to market something made from scratch, doing so in your store also sets you apart from the competition and gives your customers a reason to keep coming back for that menu item that they fell in love with and can only get at your restaurant.

As I stated in Chapter 1, the use of superior ingredients was fundamental to the pizza industry when it began in the early 20th Century. Not until the advent of chain stores did cost cutting on skimping on quality take hold. For some families, price will always be the deciding factor when ordering pizzas, but the trend is shifting back to a blend of cost and quality—somewhere in the middle between cheap chain and the high-end artisan versions.

On top of having locally sourced ingredients and scratch recipes for our pizzas, we have them for other food items on our menus, as well. Our burgers are locally sourced Angus beef and are fresh (never frozen) hand-formed patties. We offer 30-plus wing sauces that are unique scratch recipes—none come from a bottle, no way! Of course, every one of these sauces has been taste-tested and has to pass with flying colors before it lands on our menu.

Dough Handling Trends

By now you are probably getting a sense that at Caliente, there is more to preparing a pizza than laying down the dough and topping it with pre-made ingredients. I am proud of Caliente's reputation for producing "hand made" pizzas and calzones. The cooks who work for us are truly cooks who know the fine art of pizza making—pizzaiolo, if you will. They learn to make the dough that is then stored and cold fermented for 72 hours. They perfect the accepted strategies for making our sauce and chopping our veggies and other toppings. It's a skill, an art and a craft.

I'm happy to say that I've mastered a lot of dough-making techniques over the years. Usually when workers who have been in the business come to us at Caliente, they, too, have certain techniques for how they make pizza. We really like to first show new employees how we prepare each food item, starting with the dough. Once they are inside our company, we provide them with training on how to make the dough, bag the dough, store the dough and roll the dough. Then we assist them in doing all of this by helping, as needed. We will roll half of the dough and let them roll the other half. We call this our SAW approach: Show, Assist, Watch.

Innovative Menu Trends

Our search for new recipes is never ending. I guess you could say that owning a pizza shop requires both fresh ingredients and fresh ideas. Our chef continuously offers different menu options that pair with the seasonal palettes of our patrons. Like most pizza shops, we also offer sandwiches and hoagies that utilize ingredients we already have on hand, except for buns and breads. We serve other classic Italian options that customers would expect to find on the menu, such as calzones, mozzarella sticks, cheesy breads and, of course, our always popular pepperoni rolls. The deciding factors for inclusion on our menu include the popularity of the menu item and whether we find high-quality ingredients that meet our standards when producing this item.

To discover new pizza and menu trends, we use our time wisely when we attend the International Pizza Expo in Las Vegas (more about in Chapter 7) and other industry conferences. They're a great place to do research. On an ongoing basis, we also scour the pizza industry trade magazines for features that speak to pizza menu trends and spark ideas of our own. It's fun to always be pushing our edge with new menu creations. Yeah, it's a tough job but someone's gotta do it for all the pizza lovers out there!

5

Box It Up: Deliver Fun Through Brand Building, Marketing and Promotion

Early in my career at age 22, I got my first shot at being a general manager in a big franchise company that had 15 stores—four in Pennsylvania and the rest in Ohio. The store I worked at had just opened a year before I got there and the company had high hopes for big sales numbers (that they hadn't come close to realizing). At every sales meeting, the company owner would say something like:

"Art from Youngstown is up 10 percent. Let's clap for Art!"

The next meeting:

"Joe from Ashtubula is up 12 percent. Let's clap for Joe!"

Every meeting was the same. Then something happened . . .a light bulb went off in my head. On our way to one of the next meetings, I traveled in a car with the three other GMs from the Pittsburgh market— all were older than me. They spoke to me about how the supervisor wanted to fire me because my store had a dirty oven and dirty walls and they weren't sure I could lead a young team. He saw me as a kid even though I had two small children of my own at home.

That day, as I sat in the meeting and heard them talk about Mike from Geneva being up 11 percent, it clicked: SALES FIXES EVERY-THING. That night, I went to my local bookstore and bought *Guerilla*

Marketing by Jay Levinson and read it front to back. Twice. I immediately started to implement his ideas.

At the next sales meeting, the owner said:

"Nick is up 10 percent. Let's everyone clap for Nick!"

The meeting after that it was:

"Nick is up 20 percent. Let's all clap for Nick!"

And the meeting after that:

"Nick is up 44 percent. Nick, tell everyone what you're doing."

I was executing marketing methods that I learned straight from that book. I was getting involved in the community and negotiating contracts to sell pizza at the local swimming pools, football stadiums and at schools for lunches. I was applying a method of going after big customers who could add the most volume to my restaurant right away. I worked for that company long after my supervisor had left and from then on I've never forgotten that sales fixes everything.

Selling Fun

How you get those sales can be summed up in one word: Fun. One of the reasons that I am so attracted to the pizza industry is because this food item is synonymous with fun. Before McDonald's equated happiness with their now famous kid's meal, California-based Shakey's Pizza Parlor was producing advertisements that linked happiness with a slice of pizza. I still like their promotional campaign because it illustrates how pizza and smiles have been partnering for decades.

HAPPINESS
is a...

...place
called
SHAKEY'S!

If your pizza is perfection, it's SHAKEY'S!

SHAKEY'S PIZZA PARLORS

According to U.S. Department of Labor statistics, Americans' top leisure activities include watching television, hanging with family and friends, and spending time on our computers and mobile devices. Regardless of the activity, what food is most often added to increase the fun factor? Pizza! Need an inexpensive meal for your family? The answer: pizza. Need to feed your little league team after a game? Answer: pizza. Need a late-night satisfying meal after hitting the pub? Say it with me now: pizza! When there's something to commemorate, pizza's the ticket. That's why the phrase "pizza party" is so ingrained on our American culture. Pizza brings people together like no other food because it offers something to satisfy even the pickiest eaters.

And even when there's nothing special to celebrate other than being with loved ones, pizza never fails to add spice to mealtime. I'm going to make a bold statement and say that pizza actually creates family time. Statistics show that Saturday is the most popular night of the week for pizza and that's often family night. The average family eats pizza at home 30 times a year—there're only 52 weeks in the year, so that's more than once every two weeks—and this number doesn't take into consideration if the family dines out at a pizza shop. While pizza is a go-to choice for many households because it's easy to share, any leftovers are just as good the next day. (Cold pizza for breakfast? Nothing better!)

Now let's dive into some best practices for building your brand, as well as marketing and promoting your pizza business.

Brand Building Strategies

It's important to know the difference between marketing and branding. In my opinion, marketing is the way you get customers into your establishment and branding is how your customers and potential customers view your establishment. So first things first: How do you want your customers to view your brand and your establishment? What do you want to be known for? Understand that brand building is a journey that comes to fruition over time. Ideally, your customers will help guide you in determining the nuances of your brand as you gain a loyal following.

Company Logo: Your logo is going to be the first thing that speaks to what your brand is. Do you want a quirky or traditional design? Whatever style you choose makes a statement. Our logo is classy but also contemporary with both black and red neon. That wasn't always the case though. Like I said, it's been journey.

I have been very strategic about how to present the brand for Caliente Pizza & Draft House. In the beginning, I understood that I needed a logo to start building my brand and I wanted it to be fun because in my head I thought we were going to be a pick-up-and-delivery shop with a very low price point to compete with the big boys. The reason I thought that is because at that point in my career, that's what I knew. So for that first shot at our logo, I created a giant C made out of a hot pepper with a little guy who looked like a banana pepper holding a pizza. I loved that logo! Someday, I may use it as a throwback, but it wasn't true to our brand of being a full-service restaurant, which had very nice wooden back bars and hardwood floors.

One day, in a rush to get a print advertisement to a community group that we were supporting, I went outside of our store, snapped a picture of our red neon Caliente sign and sent it to the paper. When I saw our signage in that ad, I knew that the right style of logo to build our brand around had been hanging above our store the whole time.

Our original logo, which did not represent the brand we were building.

Our logo was hanging above our building all along!

Visual Collateral: Another way to drive sales is through visuals. I have done many things like set up a table by the side of the road and toss pizza dough high in the air just to call attention to the store. Over the years, you may have found me dressed up like a giant slice of pizza or a popular superhero holding a sign or banner with our current promotion's details. I also have been known to hold a sign by the side of the road that says "Honk if you love pizza!"—anything to draw attention.

Uniforms: Uniforms are another way to build your brand identity. Do you want to be a hip spot? Then maybe your employees should wear jeans. Are you going for a more upscale look? Maybe they should wear button down shirts. Maybe your brand is all about having a casual pizzeria with all organic ingredients, so tie-dye shirts may be in order. Yes, what you wear is a major part of your brand. Many employees may not understand that but it's your job to teach them about how their image affects your brand.

Brand Advertisements. In your advertising, there are times to promote and sell pizzas, and there are times to promote and sell the brand. For example, for our local school sports and musical printed programs, rather than putting in an offer for a discounted pizza, I choose to place ads that say "Good luck!" to the local sports team or "Break a leg!" to the crew of the musical. In other words, you don't always have to be selling product to get customers into your stores. In fact, building your brand is more important than selling in the beginning because later the brand will sell your pizzas.

Pizza Boxes. I can't begin to count how many pizzas I've delivered in my career. They would probably stack for miles into the sky. No matter where I've worked or what type of pizza I've delivered over the decades, one thing has never changed: The pizza box. So our best branding piece is this first thing that folks see when they order a pizza. You've got a round pizza, cut into triangles, served in a square box. Now that's geometry at its best! There are no cutting corners with this communal meal. You can slice the pie to serve a crowd and not waste a crumb. As

I said earlier, people just love it when their pizza shows up hot inside a box, the mouthwatering aroma wafting from its cardboard confines. It's inexpensive to design custom boxes. For Caliente, I chose to distinguish us from the crowd by using a black box. I inserted some strategic words and voila! Our signature Caliente pizza box was created. I think that delivering pizza in boxes is a tradition that will probably never change.

Different colors and graphics on the boxes can be fun yet all depict that same message: Good eats inside and a fun time for all who share a slice.

Our Caliente Hot Pepper Oil.

In-House, Online and On the Road Promotion: There are lots of marketing strategies that can be used in the pizza business. At Caliente, we have a systematic plan for getting our brand message known. We've even started our own brand of products with the introduction of our Caliente Hot Pepper Oil, which is great for dipping your crust into! Direct mail, social media, in-house specials and driver delivery strategies are all part of our marketing efforts.

Marketing Strategies

Trade Pizzas for PR: Trading pizzas can be a great sales tool if done correctly. I've used it with great success on several occasions. Earlier in my career when I was running a popular chain store, the local radio station called to place an order. I told them that the pizza was on the house and they responded by saying that they could not trade anything and wanted to pay for it. I insisted that it was free. I knew that they would be calling back in the future and those free pizzas would come full circle. That first time I sent the pizzas for free they sent the driver back with a couple of free CDs. The next time they called to place an order and I told them it was on the house, they gave our store an on-air mention. Word of our free pizzas got around the radio station. Eventually, their most popular DJ, Nick Nice, called in for pizza. I gave him free pies and he blasted us on the radio again.

"Big Nick from XYZ pizza over on the South Side hooked us up! Give them a call at XXX-XXXX!"

After months of giving away pizzas to the station, it finally paid off. Nick Nice told me that they wanted to thank me for the pizzas by doing a weekly on-air feature where they promoted call-ins to the station. They asked listeners to tell them why their office needed a mid-week pizza break brought to you by . . . of course, the shop I was running. This promotion went on for two years and was very successful. Nick Nice also ran a promotion where listeners could win a free 60-inch TV and a free pizza party by us. We never paid for a single bit of radio airtime and they got lots of free pizzas. It was a promotional match made in heaven!

By the way, while I'm talking about radio advertising, I want to add here that I think it is important for anybody buying any type of advertising to understand that there's always room to negotiate. One of my favorite things to do is to offer to buy a spot at a lower price, which the station will usually decline. I then suggest that the sales rep call me again at the deadline. That's most likely when I can get the advertising at my price or lower if the space is available and the rep is desperate to make that last-minute sale.

Promotion Strategies

Pizza Box and Phone Order Messages. We are selective about the messages we put on our pizza boxes. With every pizza delivery order taken, we place a menu and a box topper on each box. We average 57 carry out/deliveries per day. Over 365 days, we have handed out 20,800

The magnet that accompanies every delivery order.

menus on those boxes. When people call to place an order for delivery or pickup, we read a phone script with the daily specials. We get an average of 100 calls per day, which over the course of a year adds up to 36,500 messages.

Our box topper, which we put on every pizza box.

Contests: Creating contests and asking customers for their opinions can boost interaction at your shop. Asking "What do you think makes a great pizza?" will provide you with plenty of advice about what your next special pizza recipe might be. At Caliente, we have weekly promotions and contests that have provided continual increases in revenue while steadily expanding our customer base. Here are some examples. Each week we select a "business of the week" and provide a free meal for up to 20 people. We call the company on Monday and set a Thursday delivery. Over the course of a year, we add 52 new customer sources to our database.

Our managers also visit three businesses per week to introduce our company and give them 10 percent discount cards that are valid from 11 a.m. to 4 p.m. daily. This provides an additional 156 potential customer sources per year. We engage our staff (our phone order takers and servers) in weekly up-sale contests with prizes of free meals under $10. Adding $2 to every order taken from 900 customers (our average number of customers per week) increases sales by $1,800 per week and $93,800 per year. That's a lot of dough!

Our "Traveling Pizza Box" promotion: Take a photo with a
Caliente pizza box while on vacation and win a free pizza.

Student Specials: One pizza take-out strategy that worked well in the university section of Pittsburgh was creating a Professor Special. (It wasn't just for professors and faculty; it was for students, too!) We blanketed the university buildings with flyers that advertised the special: For any order of five or more extra-large pizzas, the price would be discounted to $11.99 each. Customers would call and order 10 Professor Specials, 30 Professor Specials, or whatever they needed depending on events happening on campus. The result? Lots of big orders with totals of more than $200 worth of pizzas on each ticket. Go after your largest potential customers with a strategic deal.

Deep Discounts. One of my early popular promotions was called Wild Wednesday: We offered medium cheese pizzas for $2.99. I advertised it with flyers on our pizza boxes for two weeks ahead of time and we placed 20 yard signs throughout the delivery area. I also spread flyers throughout the business district in my delivery area. The results were incredible: five times our normal sales in one day and a ton of new customers who tried our pizzas for the first time. I do not believe in always deep discounting your products but if you do, make an event out of it and do it only every so often.

Door Hangers: Most of you have heard of door hangers and have probably done some version of them. There's a good chance, however, that you didn't get the results you wanted but with a few tweaks and a lot of consistency, it can become an essential part of your marketing arsenal. I have three main marketing approaches that I love to employ with door hangers.

1. Your regular door hanger with an offer and four to six coupons. This brings brand awareness to your customers and keeps them current on your promotions. It finds those future customers who will try you once and if you stay in front of them after they do try you, it's your staff's job to keep them coming back. A lot of times, a customer's decision about what to have for dinner is not pre-planned. That's what makes door hanging effective. It's in-your-face marketing, as opposed to "out of sight, out of mind." Just remember that consistency is key.

2. I like to door hang with a promotion around something seasonal or local in the community. Taking this approach makes your piece more relevant to your customers' lives. I may use the schedule of local sports teams, create a holiday-themed piece or include something that will make the potential customer stop, look, read and digest the information rather than just seeing it as another pizza place giving out coupons.

3. My favorite door hanger promotion is what we call "Street of the Week." It makes the potential customer feel special and important, and it's highly effective. The content says: "Congratulations! You are the Street of the Week! This week only,

get an X pizza for X dollars! (Fill in the blank.) No limit on the number of pies!" This gives the promotion a sense of worth and urgency. It is one of my most trusted promotional tools in my toolbox.

If you want to learn about a more detailed plan on effective door hanging, feel free to email me directly.

Social Media: A philosophy that I always follow is finding a horse then beating it to death (of course, I only mean that in the figurative sense. I would never!) What I mean is this: Find what works and stick with it. Currently, that stallion is social media marketing. We use Facebook with good written content. On Twitter, we engage similar businesses by tweeting out links to our draft lists and any articles written about us. On Instagram, we focus on short videos and great photos. Social is a great way to get the word out about our promotions on a very timely basis. Things will always continue to evolve with social media and marketing in general, but consistent messaging across all media platforms should be the goal.

So there you have it—our best recommendations for internally building your brand and externally promoting it to your customers. Now let's take it a big step further and discover how your pizza shop can become a beloved and integral part of the community it serves.

6

Share a Slice of the Pie: Celebrate the Community You Serve

Without community, pizza shops cannot survive. That is why another crucial aspect of building a successful pizza enterprise is connecting with local residents, businesses, schools, charitable organizations and community-based groups. Customer loyalty is key to your success and that's why it's important to have an ongoing dialogue with your patrons. In short, your staff must view themselves as pizza shop ambassadors within your community and beyond.

Do the research and you will find that any pizza shop that's survived the test of time has no doubt made a concerted effort to create long-standing connections within their home base. With a focus on being a contributing positive factor in their community's pride, many of these shops become known as destinations within their towns. They have a beloved history with the residents, who typically think of the shop as "their" pizza hangout. When you talk to these locals, you'll hear stories of special events and good times they had while eating at these iconic locations.

We've found this to be true at each Caliente location. When we debut a store in a new location, we immediately establish relationships with the police and fire departments, as well as the pillar community organizations, to offer ways in which we can support their efforts. In many instances, this leads to special events and fundraisers that we either create or participate in. Over time, in each of our store locations, we have become known as loyal community members and not just a "business."

Staying connected with the community means keeping the lines of communication open with residents. At Caliente, we adapt the way we communicate to our residents' habits. For example, we've found that some neighborhoods like the convenience of ordering online so we offer that option on our website. Some prefer to use ride-sharing services like Uber to pick up their food rather than having it delivered so we accommodate that, as well. In other locations, we use text messaging and mobile apps. These technologies reinforce the convenience of ordering pizza and the shop's ability to serve up a tasty meal quickly.

One of the most effective ways to stay connected with the community is through social media, which we've touched on already. We post regularly about upcoming events at our shops, as well as ones that we are sponsoring in the local area. Through ongoing online dialogue, we get a sense of the residents' preferences regarding our food, service and facilities. The messages on our social platforms support daily conversations and over time, a loyal tribe has developed.

You can do the same for your shop! Following are some of our favorite community-building initiatives.

Community Support Strategies

Participate in Fundraisers. Pizza has always been a family and a kid-friendly food and, for this reason, it has become a popular way to help community groups while promoting a pizza brand. I can't stress enough that pizza shop owners who want to strengthen their community ties should consider participating in efforts such as locally based fundraisers. Community organizations have discovered that selling pizza is great for their fundraising efforts.

The formula is simple: They sell pizzas to earn some dough for their programs and the pizza shop enjoys exposure for its products. Pizza is an easy sell for all the reasons we've covered on these pages, and it's popular during any season of the year. And with how often people consume this timeless pie, it's a product they're planning to buy anyway. So using pizza products as a fundraiser is a win-win-win: for the community organization, the pizza store and the consumer. Oh, and the reward for completing the fundraising campaign? It's not unusual in many of these organizations' fundraising efforts to offer a meal in exchange for volunteer services. You guessed it! Much of the time, that meal is pizza.

Sponsor Local Sports Teams. Sports leagues of all kinds—from bowling and football to soccer and softball—wear shirts with logos from local businesses—pizza shops included. Pizza is consumed on the sidelines. Teams visit the pizza shops after a game victory to celebrate—or a loss, to make it go down easier. From the looks of it, pizza is more American (and more Americana) than apple pie!

For the past three years, Caliente has sponsored a local youth baseball league. We like to do so by providing a two-feet by three-feet banner that is displayed on the outfield wall of the ball field. The Caliente logo appears on one foot of that banner. On the remaining two feet, a graphic bulls-eye draws readers to the message: "Hit this bulls-eye to win a free pizza!" Hitting this mark in the outfield is a challenging achievement for many of the young players, but at least one hitter so far has hit the bulls-eye with a fly ball and collected his free pizza. Everyone talks about it for days afterward and even after the end of the season!

When the local Hampton Hockey Team asked us to purchase an advertisement in their team booklet, we wanted to show our support for the players. We created this advertisement:

The banner that hangs on the outfield fence at our local Little League field.

Tie Into Popular Community Events. One of our busiest times of the year at Caliente's Bloomfield location is Pittsburgh's Little Italy Days festival, where all things Italian are celebrated and sold. For four days each year, the roads close to vehicle traffic and businesses take to the streets to sell their provisions. We typically sell more than 8,000 slices of pizza at three booth locations.

Each year, Pittsburgh hosts a Craft Beer Week. This event highlights the Pittsburgh region's craft beer culture and expands the reach of craft beer through education, collaboration, cooperation and responsible libation. The event is hosted by the Pittsburgh Craft Beer Alliance, a nonprofit comprised of craft beer professionals and enthusiasts from all over the Pittsburgh region whose mission is to promote and enhance the thriving Pittsburgh craft beer scene. The inaugural Craft Beer Week was held in April of 2012. The 10-day celebration continues to grow in popularity each year. Since Caliente offers a wide variety of craft beers on our menus, this is a perfect fit for our involvement. We became a Silver Sponsor the first year, with our logo on the back of the official event T-shirts and posters.

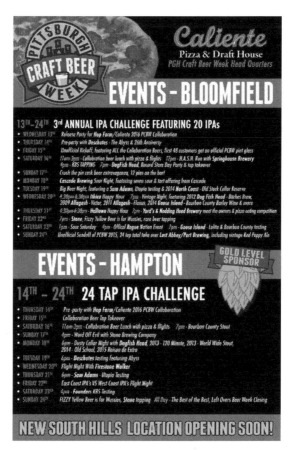

By hosting contests throughout each day of the festival that first year we were open in the Bloomfield community, we had our busiest week ever. I learned two important lessons from becoming involved in this Pittsburgh event. First, there is great importance in generating enthusiasm by hosting contests on Facebook, which, in turn, built our fan base. Having a large fan base provides us with the opportunity to promote upcoming events not just during Craft Beer Week but throughout the year. We gave away a lot of free pizzas and coupons at our stores as we generated tons of buzz online. The second thing I learned is that there is a greater following for craft beer than I had imagined. So, I dove into learning as much as I could about these specialty brews. This past year, between three of our stores, we hosted 62 events throughout Craft Beer Week. We did two a day: one in the morning and another in the afternoon. The themes were everything from "Chocolate Cake and Beer" to "Doughnuts and Beer." We tested anything we could think of. We ran an IPA Challenge featuring 20 IPAs and our fans voted for their favorites. The community loved it!

Partner with the 5K Runs. Have you heard of Hash House Harriers? In this international phenomenon, a group of people known as "Hashers" follows a cryptic trail that has been marked by the "Hare." The trail leads to beer, water, snacks and a lot of camaraderie. The spring Hasher event sponsored by Caliente occurs during the first Saturday of Pittsburgh Craft Beer Week and has a $10 entry fee and a limit of 60 participants.

One week prior to the event, a route is mapped and arrangements are made for the participants to complete the approximate 5K run. The fun run starts and ends at a Caliente location and the entry fee includes two beers along the course and two beers at Caliente. Some people run, some people walk, but they all follow these marks along streets, trails and off the beaten paths until they find a beer stop. Free pizza is provided after the run. Water and soft drinks are available but the Hashers are really known as "a drinking club with a running problem" and Caliente has become a favored partner in their fun.

All monies raised go to charity. If you sponsor such an event, consider donating the proceeds from your 5K to those in need. In addition to giving free pizza and beer to the participants, we donate $600 to our charity of choice. Over the years, we've contributed to the Multiple Sclerosis Society, American Cancer Society and the Alzheimer's Association.

Donate Gift Cards. Lots of nonprofits and community organizations ask for sponsorships and donations, as I mentioned above. We are always happy to help them in any way that we can. On rare occasions, we donate cash but we typically provide Caliente gift cards that can be raffled or used as prizes. We also create gift baskets for raffles. This approach gives folks who may not be familiar with us the opportunity to visit our stores or purchase pizza to go.

Host Holiday-Themed Events. Holiday events are another good way to become engaged in the community. We host Fourth of July celebrations at a few of our locations by setting up booths at popular street fairs. At our booths, we invite residents to taste our pizzas for the first time. We send them away with refrigerator magnets, brochures with our menu and red, white and blue balloons for the children. With so many holidays throughout the year, this is a good way for you to get totally creative with drawing both new and existing customers into your store.

Accommodate Your Clientele. Each of our five store locations serves a different community, each with its own distinct personality. The food and beverage selections and hours of operation at each location vary depending on our patrons' gastronomical tastes, beer trends and social habits. Our college-town population, for instance, prefers specific beverage selections and longer evening hours than our suburban customers.

No matter how you choose to connect with your community, always remember that doing so is a crucial part of the pizza equation—chances are, after all, that the majority of these residents are pizza lovers in search of a great slice!

PART 3:
LEAVENING BUSINESS SUCCESS THE CALIENTE WAY

7

Vegas, Baby!

One spectacular annual event marks the pinnacle of the pizza business: the International Pizza Expo in Las Vegas. This five-day extravaganza takes place in the early spring and features nine football-field-size spaces filled with vendors, competitions and educational seminars. I strongly encourage you to go if you have never been. It draws about 3,000 attendees annually. The overall theme is a sense of independent operations built upon many industry experts sharing their knowledge. This eye-opening experience has shaped how I look at running my business and always gives me an abundance of ideas to implement over the course of the coming year.

When I first traveled to the expo in 2015, I had been in business for myself for a little over a year. Seeing all things pizza-related was quite a thrill. My three managers and I we were like kids in a candy store taking in all of the vendor offerings and observing the competitions. I was amazed by these competitions, some of which are quite entertaining, like the largest dough stretch, fastest pizza stretch and fastest box folding.

Every year, the expo hosts a prestigious pizza bakeoff competition called the International Pizza Challenge. Aside from bragging rights, it offers cash prizes, a chance at winning a gold medal and the honor of being named the best in the world. The competition attracts approximately 200 pizzaioli from around the world. Each one bakes a pie on the spot from their pizza store menu and presents it to a panel of judges comprised of impartial chefs, food critics and others from the pizzeria industry. All contestants are required to bring their own ingredients. Show management provides refrigeration space, culinary equipment and ovens.

Nick on Vice Land from the World Pizza Games at the International Pizza Expo.

The bakeoff has five divisions: Traditional, Non-Traditional, Pan, Pizza Neapolitan and Roman. Entries are scored using the following criteria:

Taste is scored on:
- Crust
- Sauce, cheese, toppings
- Overall taste
- Creativity (Non-Traditional and American Pan divisions only)

Visual Presentation/ Appearance is scored on:
- Bake
- Visual presentation

That first year when I watched these competitions, I closely studied how they made the pizzas and was amazed by what pizzaiolos go through to perfect their creations. I instantly saw the marketability of winning these competitions. So we gathered many ideas and brought them back with us to incorporate into our operations. We also purchased some equipment at very good pricing—things like cooling racks, delivery bags, heat warmers, utensils and magnets that were perfect for our direct mail campaign.

We left that inaugural year feeing rejuvenated and immediately began our countdown for the following year's expo. We knew that we wanted to not just be attendees at the coming year's event; we wanted to participate its various competitions and even have a shot at winning. Yes, we had our work cut out for us, and we were excited for the challenge.

Competing at the Expo

Having worked mostly for corporate shops during my pizza career, I knew that my strength at that time was not culinary. Rather, it was that I could market with the best of them and effectively lead a team. So I got busy thinking of what I needed to do to be a viable player in the upcoming international competition. I thought of my good friend Eric Von Hansen. Eric worked as a fine dining chef in a white table-clothed restaurant and is a classically trained chef. Eric's relationship with Caliente at that point was as a culinary advisor who helped us perfect our recipes.

When I returned to Pittsburgh from that first Las Vegas Expo, the first thing I did was have Eric and his family over for dinner on a Sunday night. I pitched him on joining the Caliente staff (not just being an outside consultant) and explained to him the level of skill that was happening at the expo. I didn't want to just hire Eric so we could win competitions. After Vegas that first year, I also had an epiphany that my marriage between beer and pizza was working at such a high level of ingenuity and success that I did not want anyone to encroach on my market who had more gourmet pizza options.

Eric's initial reaction to all of this was, "Nick, that's cool but it's just pizza. I'm a fine dining chef."

I painted a future vision of world championships, more stores, vertical growth and, of course, financial gains in the way of an increased salary for these accomplishments. A few days went by then Eric called me and announced that he was putting in his 90-day notice at the restaurant where he had been an executive chef for seven years. I was elated and so excited to be partnering in this way with my talented childhood friend!

On Eric's first day on the job, we sat down and talked about what I expected and how we would grow the company. Being a believer in goals, I handed him a sheet of paper with his one-year goals. Listed on that sheet, among other things, were monthly special additions to our menus, creating an inventory system and winning the Best Pizza and World Championship at the International Pizza Expo in 2016. When Eric didn't flinch at the list, I knew I'd made the right choice in him to increase our overall food quality and really put us on the culinary map.

The year went by quickly. Eric adjusted to making pizzas and I adjusted to having a creative partner for the first time. I learned that it's a give and take. When you bring in such a high caliber employee, you need to be able to give up some control or it will never work. I was able to do just that and the relationship was working well. Ten months later, we were ready to compete in Vegas. I tried to enter Eric into the Non-Traditional Division so he could really showcase his talents (there are no limits on what a chef can create) but that division was full and taking no more entries. The other divisions have limitations on what the chefs can create so I chose the one that doesn't put restrictions on the toppings: The Pan Division. There was one catch, though: At that time, we weren't offering pan pizzas on our menus. In fact, we didn't even own a pan!

Creating "The Quack Attack"

I went to my local used restaurant equipment dealer and bought five different pans for $4 each. Eric practiced on each one until he settled on one that cooked the dough to his satisfaction. He experimented with many different creations before settling on one he loved. Being trained in French cuisine (and many others), Eric cooks a mean duck. I would often go to the restaurant where he was formerly executive chef and savor his exquisite duck dishes. It's a meal that would always leave me feeling completely satisfied.

"We have our winning recipe," Eric announced, asking me to taste-test his pizza creation. "I call it 'The Quack Attack'."
It consisted of pan seared duck, roasted garlic, butter sauce, wild mushroom ragu, fontanelle and parmesan cheeses, baby arugula, cherry tomatoes and truffle garlic oil.

"What do you think?" Eric asked as I took a big bite.

"It's exquisite. Don't do anything to it," I responded. "It tastes just like it came out of your former restaurant's kitchen."

When we arrived in Vegas that year, Eric had the same glimmer in his eye that I had the first time I attend the expo. He was in awe of everything going on in our industry. When it was time for Eric to make his pizza for the judges, he discovered that he was allowed to make two pizzas but he'd only brought one pan—the only one he owned! He made his entry in front of the judges and they appeared to be amazed by his creation. One judge grabbed a piece of the duck, tasted it slowly and closed his eyes to get the full flavor effect. We could see by the satisfied look on his face that he approved.

Later that night at the expo party where they were to announce the winner of the Pan Division, Eric was feeling a bit under the weather so he stayed back at the hotel. When they announced the winner of Best Pan Pizza in the World as Eric Von Hansen of Caliente Pizza & Draft House, we screamed in excitement and called Eric to tell him. He didn't believe us at first!

"You won the whole division! Best in the world!"

"No way! Hold on . . . I'm coming to the party!"

I called my wife and cried happy tears when I told her we'd won. She woke up the kids and I could hear their jubilation through the phone. Next, I called my parents and could hear the excitement in my mom's voice. She told Dad and he cheered in approval. I was ecstatic, as this was not only the achievement of a goal but a dream come true.

Eric came to the party and we hugged, high-fived and celebrated the moment. Then we went out on the town in a limo. There's no better place to celebrate a world championship than in Las Vegas. How do pizza guys celebrate championships? With pizza, of course! We went to the famous Tony Gemigani's Pizza Rock in downtown Las Vegas.

We now own a lot more than one pan and we sell pan pizzas on our menu using our "championship dough", along with offering "The Quack Attack." An interesting side note: When we went back to purchase more pans for our championship pizza, we told the used equipment place employees of our victory and now the pans are $32 a piece. I guess that's the price of victory.

As for Eric, he won $4,000 and a chance to compete in an Iron

Chef Challenge the next day for Pizza Maker of the Year. He finished in second place—not too shabby for a first-year pizzaiolo. I was so proud of him and our company . . . and proud of myself. We went home and ramped up our press releases and got coverage in print and broadcast news. It meant the world to me to win this competition, especially since it was on our goal list for the year and it gave us notoriety in the industry. Winning at the expo for the first time will always be one of the highlights of my pizza journey. As a result of winning this award, we are able to market our company as pizza champions and we've enjoyed a 20 percent bump in our business since then.

The excitement of that first win was contagious and we started to build a culture within the company that included our employees wanting to compete in competitions. Our goals for the coming year included winning another major championship. The general manager of our Mt. Lebanon store, Matt Hickey, had been in Las Vegas for Eric's big win. He loves handling the dough and is an expert in all things related to it. Matt was determined to also become a world champion and he set his sights on the Largest Dough Stretch competition.

Matt began to practice stretching a dough ball to the largest size he could. Every time I would go to his store during that year, he was practicing his dough stretching technique. At the Las Vegas Expo, competitors get an 18-ounce dough ball, four minutes and 50 seconds to stretch it as big as you can then 10 seconds to lay it on the ground. The floor in Matt's store had a chalk outline on it so that he could practice the entire five-minute routine from start to finish.

More Caliente Wins at the Expo

In 2017, we arrived at our third expo with seven managers and entered three competitions. Matt was ready to compete. When it was his turn to stretch the dough, you could hear the crowd's reaction. They were wowed by the size of his dough stretch: 105.4 by 99.7 centimeters. After all the flour dust had settled, Matt was a world champion and $1,000 richer. Our team was over-the-top excited. Two years in a row, we had won world championships! In the culinary competition that year, Eric won first place in the northeast Non-Traditional Division and our general manager, Nick Fink, at the young age of 21, won first place in the northeast Traditional Division. After another round of celebratory phone calls home, we piled into a "stretch" limo (appropriate, right?) and cruised down to Pizza Rock to celebrate once more.

In 2018, we returned to Las Vegas more than ready to compete and win again. After all, we were becoming seasoned competitors on this turf. That year, Eric was determined to win it all again. He had practiced relentlessly for weeks and created a Kobe beef pizza. It was incredible! Eric made it past the first round, finishing in the top position and moved onto a cook-off for first place in the Non-Traditional category. The judges watched as the remaining four competitors prepared and presented their pizzas.

Eric went last. He prepped his pizza. He heated his pan to a very high temperature and seared the beef, adding oil to the pan as flames shot up four feet high. (The smoke set off the fire alarm at the convention center!) Eric topped his freshly baked pizza with the beef. The judges where completely awed and awarded him the top prize. With that, Eric had won his second world championship and Caliente's third in a row, along with $8,000. More cheers and hugs and celebration! For me, it was mind blowing that we had just won the Super Bowl of pizza once again.

But there's more! The next day, Eric competed in the Pizza Maker of the Year and again finished second behind a very seasoned pizzaiolo from Italy. Coveting this award essentially made Eric the U.S. Pizza Maker of the Year.

On top of Eric's sensational wins, our general manager, Ozzie Turcan (a longtime friend from when I worked at his now closed Captain Pizza locations), finished second in the world and won $1,000 in the Traditional Division. Nick finished fourth in the world in the Pan Division. More happy tears, phone calls to loved ones and, of course, another limo ride to Pizza Rock to celebrate—and when we returned home, more news coverage. Caliente had officially become the "pizza of champions."

So as you can see, at Caliente Pizza & Draft House the countdown is always on for the International Pizza Expo. Our competition wins are like adding extra cheese to an already delicious pie. The friends we've gained from networking at the expo and the knowledge that my staff has acquired has been well worth the price of these trips.

For me personally, my greatest takeaway has been learning the importance of instilling pride in our Caliente team. Having outside experts recognize the quality of our work is priceless as far as morale. Our employees enjoy the recognition of being part of an award-winning organization. This ties into the overall pride that is already part of our community; after all, Pittsburgh is the City of Champions and Caliente is the pizza of champions! That winning attitude extends beyond the sports arenas and playing fields to include great food and great local businesses. We are proud to be a part of this local legacy.

The Caliente team after our big wins at the 2018 Pizza Expo.

My other greatest takeaway is the benefit of spotlighting the talent that works in our stores. By enabling our managers to represent our organization, network with other pizzerias and compete in the bake-offs and games, the morale of the entire company is boosted. Those of us who have gone to the expo have become mentors to other emerging Caliente leaders. Enthusiasm is contagious and they share the same pride in being part of a company that is a great place to work.

America's #1 Pizza Team™

When we travel to Las Vegas for the International Pizza Expo, there is always one group represented there that catches my eye: the World Pizza Champions. Once I learned about this prestigious group, it immediately became one of my goals to be named part of the team. They are highly respected and very influential in the industry. So here's how my inclusion in this coveted group of pizzaioli went down.

In 2018, after winning our third straight world championship, I received a phone call from someone I had always admired in the business: Tony Gemegiani. Tony had visited Pittsburgh back in 2014 and did a book signing for his Pizza Bible at our Bloomfield location. That was the first time I had met Tony and he was very gracious to us for hosting the event. Over the next few years, we developed a friendly relationship when we would see each other at various industry events.

With that phone call from Tony, my new goal had become realized. Tony told me that he'd been watching my progression onto the national stage, what I was doing in the Pittsburgh region and how fast we were opening up new stores. He then extended an invitation for me to be a member of the World Pizza Champions, which would recognize me as an industry expert. Even as I write this, I still get a thrill when I think about that phone call.

The World Pizza Champions™, America's #1 Pizza Team™, are made up of founding members Tony Gemignani, Michael Shepherd, Siler Chapman, Joe Carlucci, Ken Bryant and Sean Brauser. It also includes many other members from around the globe. Our team is built from a diverse crowd of independent pizza operators who have a true passion for pizza and preserving the art of real pizza making.

True to our name, our members have earned countless gold medals, accolades and awards at pizza competitions globally in numerous categories of Pizza Acrobatics and Pizza Baking, proving that we truly are world champions of not just pizza games and pizza acrobatics, but pizza making, as well. From the back-to-back wins in the Team Acrobatic Competition at the World Pizza Championships in Salsomaggiore, Italy to the *Guinness Book of World Records*, all the way to the Triple Crown win of Tony Gemignani in Naples, Italy, we hold more medals and awards than any other pizza team in the world.

Our team members have appeared on Oprah, The Today Show, The Tony Danza Show, The Tonight Show, The Ellen Show, ESPN, Food Network, The Discovery Channel, Rachel Ray Show, Emeril Live, Good Morning America, The Early Show, ABC, CNN, BBC, RAI, *Sabato Gigante,* and more. You can also find us performing acrobatic dough-throwing shows around the world at numerous festivals, fairs, sporting events and food shows. It is an honor to be a part of this esteemed team. It has brought my career as a pizza entrepreneur full circle, just like our pizzas!

8
Washing It Down: The Craft Beer Phenomenon

Craft brewers are a lot like pizza aficionados: Both are passionate and borderline fanatical about their areas of specialty. Both use fresh ingredients and employ creativity in perfecting their chosen form of art. Both toil endlessly so their customers can savor the taste sensations. So why not blend the two?

As I've mentioned already, I didn't know anything about craft beer and the specialty beer industry when I bought my first store and inherited an established bar. The extent of my beer knowledge was about Heineken, Rolling Rock, Miller Lite and Sam Adams. Because I had the attitude with my first shop that I would not fail no matter what, it was super important that I master the bar business. I established a plan to learn all I could as quickly as possible.

Learning the Bar

Working 18-hour days in those early years, there wasn't much time to do industry research but for a solid year when I went home at night, rather than watching sports, I'd do online research. I scoured brewery websites and read about their different styles of beer. I discovered that a lot of craft brewers humbly began their ventures as hobbyists and home brewers out of their garages then decided to scale their businesses. I became friends with a local brewer, Matt Moninger, who kindly taught me about the styles and perplexities of various beers. He later became our first bar manager and his contributions to our team since joining us have been significant. On any day of the week, you can find Matt at one of our locations training and teaching our staff about craft beer.

I also befriended my local beer sales rep, who was a beer enthusiast willing to teach me what he knew about the craft beer industry. In addition, I studied the reality TV series "Bar Rescue" with Jon Taffer. Not everything in the show was helpful but I've applied a lot of tips that I learned from it, such as not changing the Caliente name. (We changed it from Caliente Pizza & Bar to Caliente Pizza & Draft House about nine months after purchasing it.)

I also did legwork by researching the most popular bars in my city to see what they where doing. I noticed the trend of craft beer right away. Most had a popular beer and a specialty one-off beer on tap that people would talk about and, better yet, travel to drink it. Once I located the good local bars, I started taking my family out to dinner every Wednesday evening (my only evening off) for reconnaissance. After about a month or so, my kids wanted to know if our weekly family night out had to be at a bar! I studied every detail. What was on their beer list? Was it extensive or niche? Which ones were on tap? How did they serve the beer? How did they price it? What type of coolers did they store it in? What signage did they create about the beers? What lighting did they use to showcase their beer selections? How many bartenders were working on an average evening? I learned many things that all the bars where doing the same. I noted these best practices. I also saw some things that some bars did better than others. I noted those, as well.

Before we bought Caliente, I had maybe in my lifetime been in only a dozen or so bars and definitely not that many beer bars. Since I have owned Caliente, I have visited hundreds of beer bars all over the country on the quest for even better business practices. I've found new ways to write our draft lists, price and serve our beers, and design our spaces.

One bar even inspired our black walls; when I came back from a New Jersey trip, painted the whole store black and my staff walked in, the looks on their faces faces were priceless! Even though I consider us a restaurant more than a great craft beer bar, I have gained great knowledge from all of those visits and have successfully combined them into a great craft beer restaurant.

Bringing in Specialty Brews

Pittsburgh is a small city in comparison to places like Philadelphia, where the craft beer business was already firmly established by the time I opened Caliente. I set out to visit other cities and learn more about how the industry was evolving nationally. In doing so, I was exposed to a wider variety of products and general knowledge. For example, I learned that serving beer in an appropriate glass is important for bringing out its aroma, taste and texture. I noticed that the draft selections were always changing as new beers became available. In larger markets, smaller breweries would ship their products to their chosen establishments. A small brewery in California, for instance, would sell their beer in California and pick two other places in the United States to offer their "limited supply" of beer. They would most likely choose larger cities like Philly that had bigger beer-drinking populations.

I quickly realized that getting craft brewers' specialty beers to Pittsburgh would be a challenge because they required us to sell their basic beer product for a year before they would commit to making their specialty craft brews available to us. So I devised an idea: What if I brought beer from Philadelphia to Pittsburgh so that my customers could enjoy that "limited supply" California brew? It would be an exclusive beer because no other Pittsburgh bars were establishing relationships with these Philly-based bars. Our customers would be getting beers that they couldn't get anywhere else in the 'Burgh.

So that's what I did. I figured out what license I would need to transport beer from Philadelphia to Pittsburgh and hired an individual who had a license to transport alcohol. He would load up his vehicle in Philadelphia with 20 or 30 kegs and cases of beer and then drive it across the state. Talk about special delivery! I remember thinking, *Okay, after we put all this beer in our stores, it's only a matter of time before it catches on that we've got the best beer in Pittsburgh.* Now, the scale was tipped in our favor. In a short amount of time, we went from using a van to bring in specialty cases to having breweries banging on our doors to sell their products directly. We created a crazy good buzz at Caliente and our local market took notice that ours was the place to find craft beers that are not available anywhere else in the city.

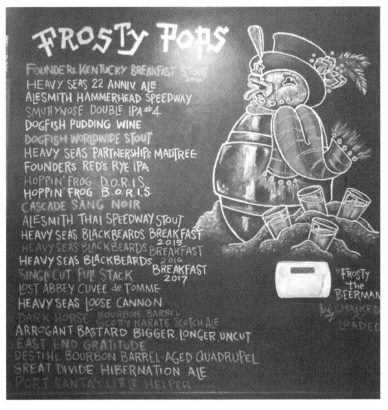

The beer list at the Caliente Bloomfield store.

At Caliente, we continue to create an atmosphere for beer enthusiasts who enjoy fresh new brews. We like to earmark Friday nights to host talks from local head brewers, and our clientele come in and sample whatever beer he has just created. Every week, we select the beer specials, usually working one month in advance to thoughtfully make these selections. The specials may be seasonal, such as a pumpkin beer during the fall season, or a Christmas in July beer special in July. Typically, a beer representative from outside the Pittsburgh region will be in

A collaboration beer that we brew annually with a local brewery.

attendance to share his knowledge about his particular brews, and there are usually free pint glasses all around after the presentation.

In addition, wholesale distributor representatives and local craft beer brewery representatives usually visit Caliente on a weekly basis. When there is a new product that a rep wants to promote, it is not unusual for us to highlight that beer as our Friday night special. Our customers love it and our reps love it, too!

A Firkin Craze

As we continued to study the craft beer industry, we discovered something called a Firkin, a real ale with no carbonation that's served in pubs in England. Some craft brewers in the U.S. take the beer that they make in a tank with no oxygen or carbonation and fill it with exotic fruits like pomegranates, more hops and stuff like mint-chocolate-chip cookies to give it

Our annual release at the Firkins event.

various flavors. These flavored beers are usually brewed in one-off runs.

96

When we discovered Firkins, we'd already had very limited supplies of beer coming in from Philadelphia and local beer distributors were banging on our doors for us to serve what they had in stock. Now we could add to the mix locals who were making Firkins. Some of their batches were so limited that when we tapped them on the bar, the Firkin would be empty in five hours or less.

I am a lifelong learner in the beer industry because it is always evolving. In fact, for a while, I had to put my pride in knowing the pizza industry so well on the back burner. I had to trust my staff to run the back end of the pizza shop while I grew our craft beer business.

In the end, my passion for great pizza and now the best craft beer is what makes this food-beverage partnership work so deliciously. In fact, the most common thing that our beer customers say when they order from our food menu is, "Wow! This isn't typical bar food. The pizza is amazing!"

9
The Caliente Recipe for Success

The way in which I purchased my restaurants is unique so I'd like to share a bit about that process, as well as give my take on the other things that have solidly led to our success.

I mentioned earlier about our four-day store turnaround and now I'd like to expand on that. Having watched a lot of the "Bar Rescue" reality TV show as part of my research on how to run a bar, I'd become fascinated with the process of taking over and flipping a bar or restaurant in less than a week. The way I have structured all my deals is to have the existing owner keep his establishment open until the Sunday before we take over; then we do so on a Monday and by Friday at four o'clock, we are open with a new name, new concept and a fresh look.

How is this possible? As I will share below, I do not believe in extensive planning, just massive action. That Monday, we come in with a quick idea of what we want the end result to be and we work towards it. When buying an existing business, you are acquiring everything from the light fixtures to flooring so we try to use as much of these existing items as possible. Manpower is key here. We coordinate plumbers, electricians, handymen, friends and family to take part in this massive undertaking—everything from total gutting and repairs to cleaning. We have found this process to be so rewarding that we now crave and love taking over someone else's bar of how many years and turning it into a Caliente restaurant for years to come. This process proves that if you think you can, you can!

The Caliente Aspinwall store under construction.

The Mt. Lebanon store before the takeover.

Cash vs. Finance

Many assume that when you set out to start a business, your first step is to visit a banker to put together a business loan. I took another approach. First, I want to dispel the myth that you need to have a lot of money up front. My business growth strategy has been to put money down instead of financing my ventures. I have found that if you have some cash to use as hand money, you can buy a store without needing all the monies at once. This way, I have been able to leverage risk, my hard work and the seller's pain into the purchase of shops at reasonable prices.

Sorting the wall signs for the Mt. Lebanon store.

You'd be surprised at that person who has their cousin running a shop or the owner who was unfortunately hit with a life hardship or is simply burned out. When the owner has no other viable offers and you put a cash offer on the table, things tend to look a little different. In many cases, having this option is a blessing and a huge relief for the owner who no longer wants the burden of carrying the business. You can offer, as an example, a lump sum up front—say, $50,000 or $75,000— then pay an established monthly amount with interest for five years.

We always use a business attorney to write the contract with the promissory note, and as long as I pay everything on time, I own everything from the moment I sign the contract. The beauty of this purchasing agreement is that I am buying the store as it is currently operating with all of the fixtures included so we can hit the ground running. This process is favorable for the former owners as well because it allows them to literally walk away from the business with cash in hand and no further concerns or problems.

Finding Gems vs. Starting a New Business

Essentially, I was able to acquire my restaurants this way partly because I was buying someone else's "weakness." What I mean is that I sought out individuals who'd been running their shops for years and were either burned out or looking to get out as soon as possible, not someone trying to "cash out" and retire to Florida. In each of these scenarios, the negotiations are different. If somebody is looking to retire, they're usually asking for a larger buyout amount because they know how hard they've worked building the value in their business.

This is not the case if the owner is burned out and looking for a way to exit. This type of owner cares less about the buyout amount and more about being able to retire the business. It may be someone who thought they had this great investment and could simply enlist a relative or friend to run the store and keep the cash flow going. That generally doesn't work. These individuals are good candidates for a buyout at a lower price.

When buying our stores, we sought out businesses that were busy at one time and had life. For example, our first store was called Gators back in the Eighties and Nineties. It was popular then and the owners made a healthy profit for a neighborhood pub-style bar. The subsequent owners did not fare as well and by 2012 the business was dying. It needed someone to put it on life support, which is what we did.

The Aspinwall store on opening night.

The history of our Hampton store was somewhat similar to our Bloomfield store. In the Nineties, it was called Bob's Wings and Six Packs. It was a popular place to get good wings, good fried food and a variety of beers. Locals would come in when football games were on the TV and there'd be a line of people ordering different flavors of wings. Again, when new owners took it over, the business sank and the store didn't have the same pizzazz it once had.

Our Mt. Lebanon store was also a very popular pub and pizza shop in the Eighties and Nineties. It hosted many birthday parties, family celebrations and community events. Once again, the new owners were not able to sustain the previous success. This store was dying to be brought back to life. Again, we resuscitated the business and it was a hit because people remembered enjoying it in years past.

Mom, Dad, brother and family supporting us on
opening night in Mt. Lebanon.

Similarly, our fourth store had been a popular place in the Nineties that people would frequent after work. Customers loved the happy hour and good food. When the owner, who initially established this restaurant, moved his business to a new location, no one was able to replace his success at the original location. Yet, when we opened it as our fourth Caliente Pizza & Draft House, the clientele reappeared and they've stayed with us ever since.

Looking back, I can say that one of things we do well is identify those business gems that have lost their luster. We flip them with new ownership, build a solid team, add our special touch of pizazz and watch the bottom line swing upward as we win back a loyal customer base.

The Caliente Hampton store.

Plan vs. Improvise

Another thing that many people assume they need when starting a business is a formal business plan. I took a different approach on that, as well. The need for a business plan depends on the type of person you are. For me, quick decision-making and drive are more important than drafting a traditional plan. I believe that a true entrepreneur has to have a main skill of improvisation to go along with his or her overall vision.

What do I mean by that? Well, as much planning as you do—whether it's having an inspector add more steps or hiring enough staff to open—many things will not go the way you intend when actually running the business. The way I open up stores is with a clear mind and a vision of the opened restaurant as a success based on where my hunches are taking me. Sometimes my plan changes day to day, depending on the circumstances.

One main way in which we improvise is around how we upgrade our restaurants. We may think we know what we want to do but once we get in there and put a fresh coat of paint on the walls, the rest of it starts to become clear. The upgrades that we may have thought we needed to do to a space may not be necessary once the rehab starts.

The repainted awning that saved us $30,000.

Oftentimes, problems can be worked around by going with the flow of things. For example, while opening our third restaurant, we were left with a giant blue awning with lights. Our original idea was to remove it and put up our custom neon sign like we had at our other two locations. Well, we couldn't have anticipated what came next: When we applied at the township office for a permit to put up the sign, they informed us that if we took down the awning, the hood fan on the other side of that awning would no longer be grandfathered in. That meant it would have to be moved to the roof at an additional expense of $30,000.

Wanting to open in a few days and not seeing the value of moving the fan, we made a quick decision. We had a painter come out and put three coats of paint on the sign then our sign guy created large letters to be placed on the awning. So instead of the potential $40,000 cost to move the hood fan and replace the sign—which would not have been in our business plan had we written one—the painting and lettering came in at $900. Three years later, this awning still looks as attractive as the day we painted it and the best part is that the hood fan is still there and working fine.

To sum it up, our family motto is "Make It Happen."

Surround Yourself With Great People

None of my success with Caliente would have been possible with the most important resource: great people. Being able to communicate your vision as an entrepreneur and operator to the people around you is crucial. Getting others to share your vision and see the opportunities it can provide for them is key. And yet using these skills extends beyond just your staff. It's also important to surround yourself with solid professionals who can support you in meeting your goals; for example, a good lawyer who specializes in your field, a liquor attorney for liquor transactions, a real estate attorney for land deals, a trusted CPA, an insurance broker who can shop your coverages and update your policies based on your needs throughout the years. The relationships you have with your vendors is crucial and you'll need reliable plumbers, electricians, HVAC experts and oven repairmen to keep your equipment up and running.
I look for three things when I am putting this group together: 1) Do they call me back and do they do what they say what they are going to do? 2) Are they fair not just in price but in making something right so you can keep your restaurant open? 3) Do they have integrity and do they display your same core values such as honesty and strong work ethic?

Take Big Risks vs. Play it Safe

No risk, no reward. Perhaps you have heard this phrase before. For me, it is a matter of truth. When I started Caliente, as you will recall, I was running one store and working as a postman—essentially two full-time jobs. I was making $70,000 between those two jobs and I walked away from that salary and took a chance that what I had done for others along the way I could do for myself. On top of that, I was about to take on a huge amount of debt.

Most people probably think about the financial risk when opening a business but the other risk you take relates to all the people who work for you. You also take ownership of the fact that they and their families count on you to succeed. This responsibility can weigh on your mind but I focused on the reward of being able to do what I love. Of course, all the other things that come with success are nice but for me it was and is more about my passion for pizza and doing it for myself.

For me, risk is the power that fuels my entrepreneurial journey. Every time we open a new location, we also open up the door to risk. Financially speaking, I do not need to open more stores but the rewards that these new stores offer are far greater than the risk—the best reward is being able to offer more jobs and opportunities for the employees who have helped me along the way.

Know What Success Means to You

When I first started Caliente, I mistakenly thought that I would be successful whenever three things occurred:
1. I could purchase a car that wasn't from the last century. Until then, I had always only driven $500 cars or hand-me-downs until they died.
2. I could save for and afford to pay for my two children's eventual college educations.
3. My family and I could move into a bigger house.

These are three very personal reasons but at that time, it was how I would have judged my success. After a year of Caliente, I realized that I was going to be able to do all three of those things. That is when I started to understand that achieving them wasn't how I would define success. I instead began to define it by my employees being able to do those things for themselves and their families. To this day, this is what drives me as I continue to grow Caliente.

Think Positive and Focus on Goal Setting

A belief system that I can attribute my success to is focusing on the positives and not the negatives. Either is always an option and I chose to look for positives in any given situation. Another factor in my success, which goes hand in hand with positive thinking, is goal setting. By that I don't mean ideas in your head. Those are dreams! Goals must be written down. There is power in the pen. Begin with writing one-year, three-year, five-year and 10-year goals, along with why each goal is a worthy one. Then visualize yourself accomplishing each goal.

I recently rediscovered one of my early goal sheets that got packed away when we moved into a new home. To my surprise and delight upon rereading it, most of my goals from seven years ago had come to reality. Tears came to my eyes! One of those goals was to be on the cover of Pizza Today magazine. In October 2018, that happened! Caliente's pepperoni pizza graced the cover of an issue celebrating the top 100 independent pizzerias in the industry (we were included on that list for the second straight year). Seeing our pizza on the cover reestablished for me that I am not just reaching for invisible dreams but rather achieving tangible goals.

Write down your goals and watch the "power in the pen."
Here's our pepperoni pizza on the cover of Pizza Today
Magazine 2018.

Take One Bite at a Time

One of my mantras in life and business—and even in writing this book—has been:

"How do you eat an elephant? One bite at a time!"

I have a life-size replica of an elephant's head above my office desk to remind me of this. I believe in taking small bites every day—not just of pizza but toward your goals—then looking back when they're reached and admiring the massive results. You, too, can have what I have. You must be willing to be patient and put in the hard work. Success is not an overnight phenomenon. Grow your business steadily over time and learn at each step along the way. Take all those lessons acquired into your next job or venture. Keep reading and exploring everything you can about our industry, and above all else, have fun doing it!

I hope that in reading this book you've picked up on my passion for pizza and what this great industry has meant to me. I tried to pack these chapters with stories of encouragement and some tried-and-true tips. When I look back at my journey in this great industry for the past 23 years, I feel many different emotions. There is definitely a sense of accomplishment that a kid who started as a delivery driver at age 17 could fall in love with the teamwork and challenges of the pizza industry and dedicate his working life to becoming an industry leader. That's what I love about this industry; no matter where you are, there is always a need for a great pizza and if you have the work ethic and passion, anything is possible.

My dream was always to have my own shops (notice the plural). When I worked at my first job as a teenager, that company had 46 stores in the Pittsburgh market. When I left them five years later, they had 123 stores. Since then, I have always believed that this type of growth is possible. Many people ask me if I saw myself opening the five shops that I have and I respond, "Yes, I did, and I see many more in the future."

Not a day goes by when I'm not thankful to be living out my dream. It's the classic American dream. Some people believe that the American dream is dead but I am here to tell you that it is alive and well for many of us in the pizza industry. We are living proof! And we're not going anywhere for the foreseeable future—at least, not as long as pizza continues to do that thing it does best: bring people together to create their own big delicious slice of happiness.

Resources for Success

BOOKS

Growing Pizza, Michael Shepard
Guerilla Marketing, Jay Levinson
How to Win Friends and Influence People, Dale Carnegie
Jab Jab Jab Right Hook, Gary Vaynerchuk
Profits in the Pie, Scott Anthony
The Compound Effect, Darren Hardy
The Entrepreneur Roller Coaster, Darren Hardy
The Four-Hour Work Week, Tim Ferris
The Pizza Bible, Tony Gemignani
The Power of Focus, Jack Canfield, Les Hewitt and Mark Hansen
The Ultimate Sales Machine, Chet Holmes
Think and Grow Rich, Napoleon Hill
Who Moved My Cheese, Spencer Johnson

WEBSITES

Pizzatoday.com
PMQ.com

PODCASTS

The Smart Pizza Marketing Podcast
"The Secret" (2006 film, available on Netflix)

Caliente's Pizzeria Awards

2013
- Best New Pizza Restaurant voted by WPXI-TV Pittsburgh

2015
- Best Pizza in Bloomfield Readers' Choice Awards, *Pittsburgh Tribune-Review*
- Thrillist, Best Bar in Pittsburgh
- Thrillist, Best Late Night Eats
- Gold for Best Pizza in the City, Readers' Choice Awards, *Pittsburgh Tribune-Review*
- Named Rogue Brewery's Pittsburgh Embassy
- Named in the book Mid-Atlantic Beer Lovers Best Breweries, brew pubs and beer bars

2016
- Best Pan Pizza in the World, International Pizza Expo, Las Vegas, Nevada
- Thrillist, Best Pittsburgh Bar With Best Late Night or Anytime Eats
- Gold for Best Pizza in the City, Readers' Choice Awards, *Pittsburgh Tribune-Review*
- Gold for Best Pizza in the North Hills, Readers' Choice Awards, *Pittsburgh Tribune-Review*
- Gold for Best Hoagies in the North Hills, Readers' Choice Awards, *Pittsburgh Tribune-Review*

2017
- 1st place, East Division Traditional Pizza at the World International Pizza Expo
- 1st place, East Division Non-Traditional Pizza at the World International Pizza Expo

- Gold for Best Pizza in Pittsburgh, Readers' Choice Awards, *Pittsburgh Tribune-Review*
- Gold for Best Wings in the City, Readers' Choice Awards, *Pittsburgh Tribune-Review*
- Gold for Best Pizza in Bloomfield, Readers' Choice Awards, *Pittsburgh Tribune-Review*
- Gold for Best Pizza in the North Hills, Readers' Choice Awards, *Pittsburgh Tribune-Review*
- Named to *Pizza Today*'s Hot 100 Independent Restaurants

2018
- Best Non-Traditional Pizza in the World, International Pizza Expo, Las Vegas, Nevada
- Named to *Pizza Today*'s Hot 100 Independent Restaurants

Caliente Pizza & Draft House locations:

4624 Liberty Avenue, Pittsburgh, PA
329 Castle Shannon Boulevard, Pittsburgh, PA
225 Commercial Avenue, Pittsburgh, PA
4706 William Flynn Highway, Allison Park, PA
2125 Mosside Boulevard, Monroeville, PA

Acknowledgements

I express my sincere thanks to Dr. Ann Gatty, who kept telling me that my story needed to be told and pushed me to share it.

I pay a deep sense of gratitude for the many managers and colleagues who have helped shape a young kid into a man who wanted to succeed in this industry—including but not limited to Ufuk Kesser, Jim Fitzsimmons, John Herazo, Joe and Colleen Cuda, the late Jeff Clegg, Steve Crum, Chuck Lake, Seth Goldhardt, Danny Savurdich, Victor Rajasa, Ozzie Turcan, Paul Powell, Jeremy Galvin, Sam Big Dog Holmes and Michael Staunton.

Thank you to my friend Jimmy Dargocey for his encouragement throughout the years. May we always keep going after our dreams.

In this day and age, rarely does a handshake and someone's word mean something. I'm eternally grateful to Taner Nalbant and Danny Shah for keeping their word and shaking my hand.

The world is a better place thanks to people like Greg Parrotto who want to develop and lead others. His insights and mentorship along this journey have been priceless. Thank you.

I'm grateful to have great entrepreneurs in my life like my Uncle Jim and Aunt Debbie Bogacz. As a young boy, I always watched them and wanted to grow up and be just like them.

A debt of gratitude is owed to Tony Gemignani for the humbleness and teacher-like qualities he shows to anyone in the industry who shows a sincere interest in bettering themselves through their love and passion of pizza.

Sincere thanks to Scott Anthony for driving an hour and a half to taste the pizza of some guy who won some award. Thanks for inviting me to my first pizza expo and showing me the light of the independent pizza industry.

A hearty thanks to Nino Sunseri for letting me be a student to his ways and always sharing his wisdom and guidance with me.

Thank you Eric Von Hansen—my friend, my Regional Chef and fellow World Pizza Champions team member—for many things, including always listening to my ideas then bringing them to life, and for not letting us use fake butter.

I want to acknowledge my editor, Gina Mazza, for her guidance and truly pulling the "rest" of the story out of me, and to my illustrator, Lee Ann Fortunato-Heltzel, for putting my story into pictures and graphics.

A HUGE thank you to all my employees past and present at Caliente Pizza & Draft House. Without their hard work and dedication, none of this would be possible. One Team, One Dream!

I owe a great many thanks to my children, Lilly and Perry, for always listening to me talk about work and taking that phone call, and for always believing in the "Fosh."

I could write another whole book only about the unconditional love and support that my parents, Bill and Eileen Bogacz, have always had for all their children, including me. Thank you, Mom and Dad, for endless hours of flash cards and for always listening.

Last but not least, gratitude to my wife, Angie Bogacz, my #1 cheerleader and supporter, who never let me give up on my dream. This book is as much hers as it is mine.

About the Author

Nick is the President/Founder of Caliente Pizza & Draft House. With more than 20 years of experience in the industry, he opened his first location in fall of 2012 and has grown quickly to his five current locations. Nick started in the industry as a delivery driver in 1996 and fell in love with the team atmosphere and high energy that the pizza business provides.

Working his way through many levels of corporate chain pizza companies, he always had his eye set on opening his own independent stores. Nick loves the freedom an independent operation provides for company decision-making. He is a motivating leader and team builder and has grown his company to more than 185 employees through leading by example.

Caliente team members have won numerous awards in the industry, including World Championships at the Las Vegas Pizza Expo. Nick is also a part of the International Pizza Expo's family of speakers.
Nick was successful in bringing together pizza and craft beer within his company. Each of his restaurants boasts over 24 taps and a bottle selection of more than 150 beers. His stores specialize in hard-to-source craft beers from across the country and around the world. He has also taken a unique approach to craft beer by setting up collaboration brews with breweries.

Nick's goals in the pizza industry continue to be met by being committed to excellence with focus and positive vibes. His wife, Angie, has been his biggest supporter and is proud to be a Pizza Wife for Life. Their teen-aged children have grown up in the industry and have taken a keen interest in the business. When not in the grind and everyday hustle that he craves, Nick enjoys having fun and relaxing with his family.

Nick can be reached at pizzadrafthouse@gmail.com.

Manufactured by Amazon.ca
Bolton, ON

13022839R00068